MS Word

Davinder Singh Minhas

RISING SUN

an imprint of
New Dawn Press

NEW DAWN PRESS GROUP
New Dawn Press, Inc., 244 South Randall Rd # 90, Elgin, IL 60123
e-mail: sales@newdawnpress.com
New Dawn Press, 2 Tintern Close, Slough, Berkshire, SL1-2TB, UK
e-mail: ndpuk@newdawnpress.com
sterlingdis@yahoo.co.uk
New Dawn Press (An imprint of Sterling Publishers (P) Ltd.)
A-59, Okhla Industrial Area, Phase-II, New Delhi-110020
e-mail: sterlingpublishers@touchtelindia.net
Ghai@nde.vsnl.net.in

© 2005, New Dawn Press

All rights are reserved. No part of this publication may be reproduced, stored in a retrieval system or transmitted, in any form or by any means, mechanical, photocopying, recording or otherwise, without prior written permission of the publisher.

Printed at Sterling Publishers Pvt. Ltd., New Delhi

Contents

1. Introduction — 5
2. Creating Documents — 12
3. Editing the Text — 19
4. Formatting the Text — 31

1. Introduction

You can create, process and revise your document such as letters, resumes and reports with the help of Word, which is a full-feature word processing program. To create high-quality brochures, advertisements and newsletters, you can use Word's desktop publishing features. There are many tools provided by Word that enable you to create Web pages and place these Web pages directly on a Web server.

The various features of Word like borders, shading, tables, graphics, pictures and Web addresses can be included in the documents. You can instruct Word to create a template, which is a form you can use and customize as per your requirements. With proper hardware, you can dictate text instead of typing it into Word.

You can also send a copy of your Word document to E-mail addresses when connected to the Internet. While you type in a variety of languages, Word can detect the syntax errors. Word's thesaurus allows you to add a variety and precision to your writing. Word can also format text such as headings, lists, fractions, borders and Web addresses as you type them.

Functions of Word

Edit Document: Word offers many time-saving features like add, delete and rearrange to help you edit text in a document. You can also count the number of words in a document and check your document for spelling and grammar errors.

Format Document: You can format the document in order to enhance its appearance. Various fonts, styles and colors can be used to emphasize important text. You can also adjust the spacing between lines of the text, change the margins, centralize text on a page and create newspaper columns.

Drag and Drop Series

Tables: To neatly display columns of information in a document, Word can help you create tables. Word's ready-to-use designs allow you to instantly give the table a professional appearance.

Graphics: Graphics, such as AutoShapes, Clip Art images and diagrams can be added to a document to illustrate ideas.

Mail Merge: To produce personalized letters for each person on a mailing list, Word's Mail Merge Wizard can be used. This is useful if you often send the same document, such as an announcement or advertisement, to many people.

Starting and Customizing Word

To start Word, Windows must be running. Perform the following steps to start Word:

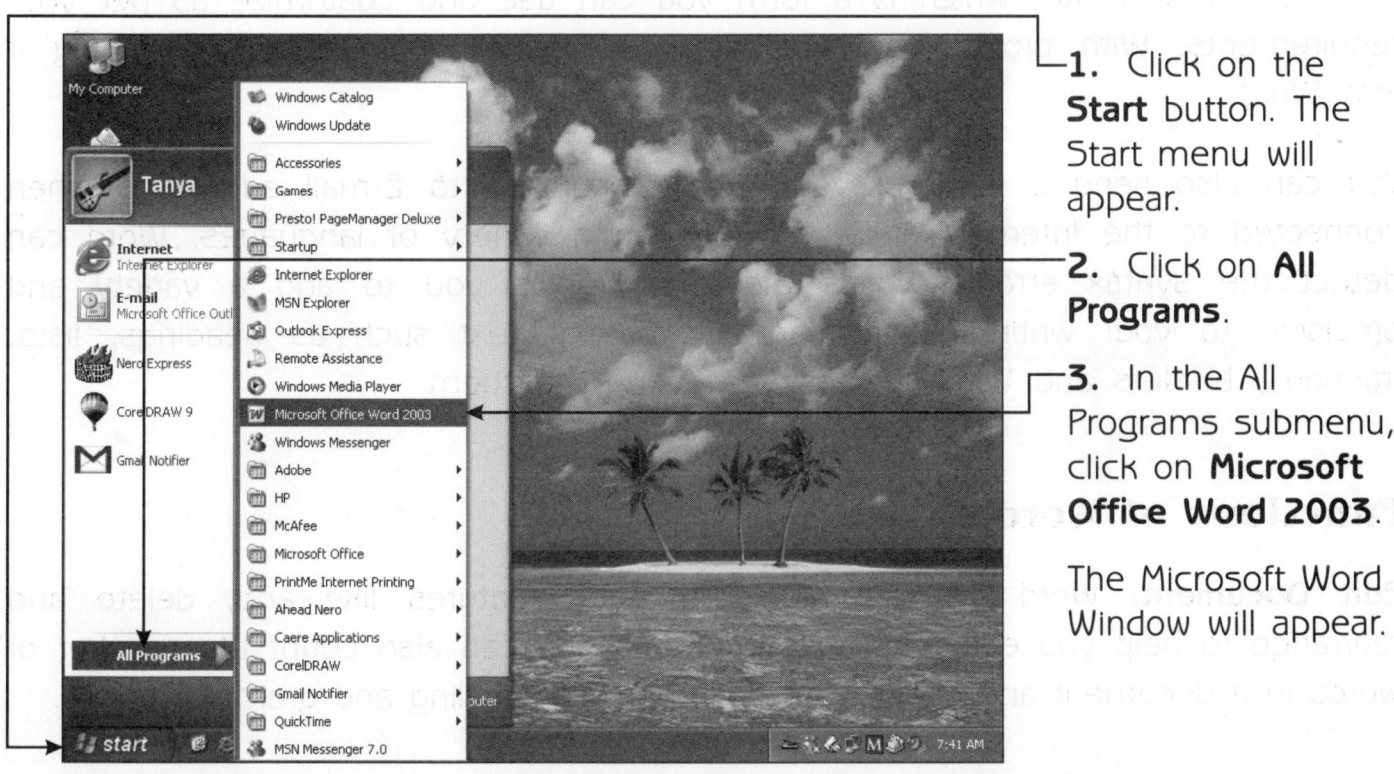

1. Click on the **Start** button. The Start menu will appear.

2. Click on **All Programs**.

3. In the All Programs submenu, click on **Microsoft Office Word 2003**.

The Microsoft Word Window will appear.

*(In some versions of Windows, you have to click on **Programs** in place of **All Programs** to start Word.)*

6

Word

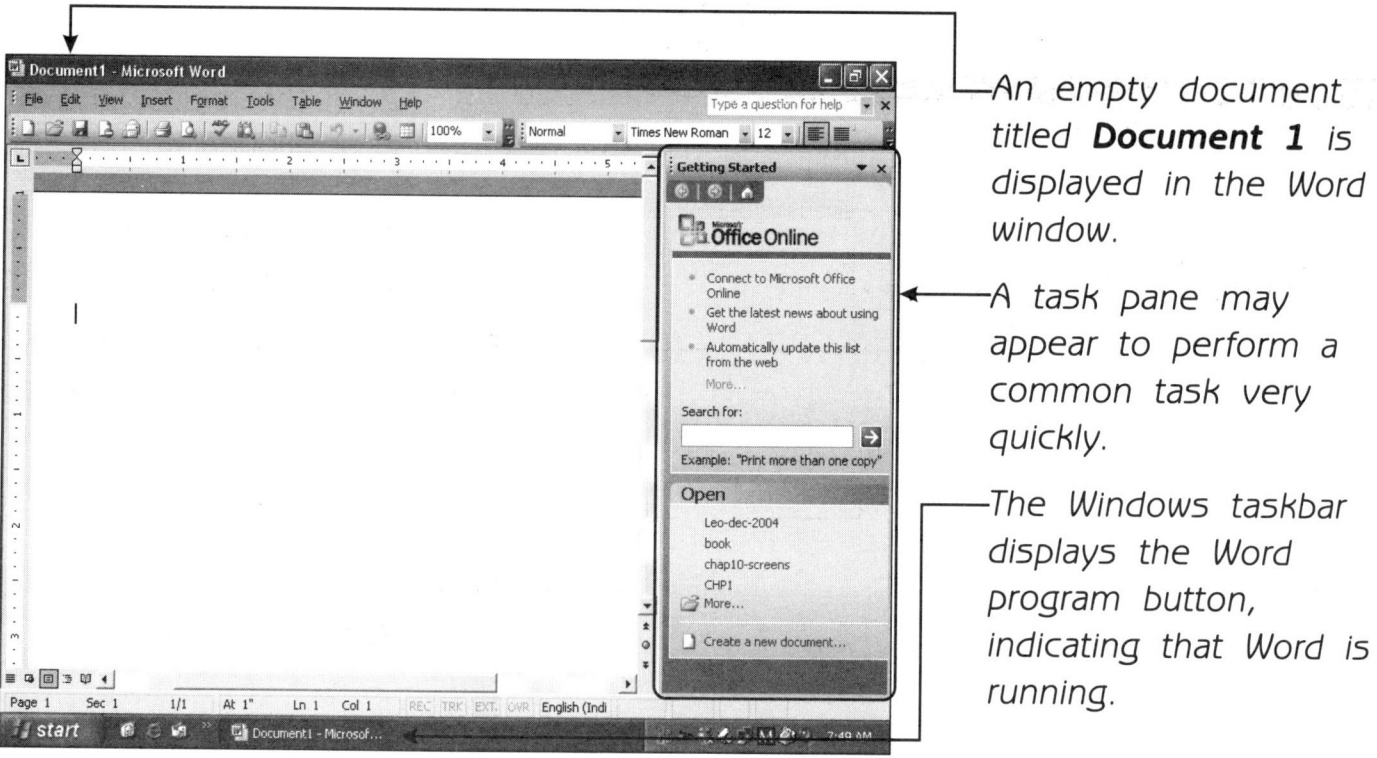

— *An empty document titled **Document 1** is displayed in the Word window.*

— *A task pane may appear to perform a common task very quickly.*

— *The Windows taskbar displays the Word program button, indicating that Word is running.*

To allow maximum typing area in Word, the task pane may be closed down. For more efficient use of the buttons of the toolbar, they should be displayed in two separate rows instead of sharing a single row. To close the New Document task pane and display the toolbar buttons in two separate rows, perform the following steps:

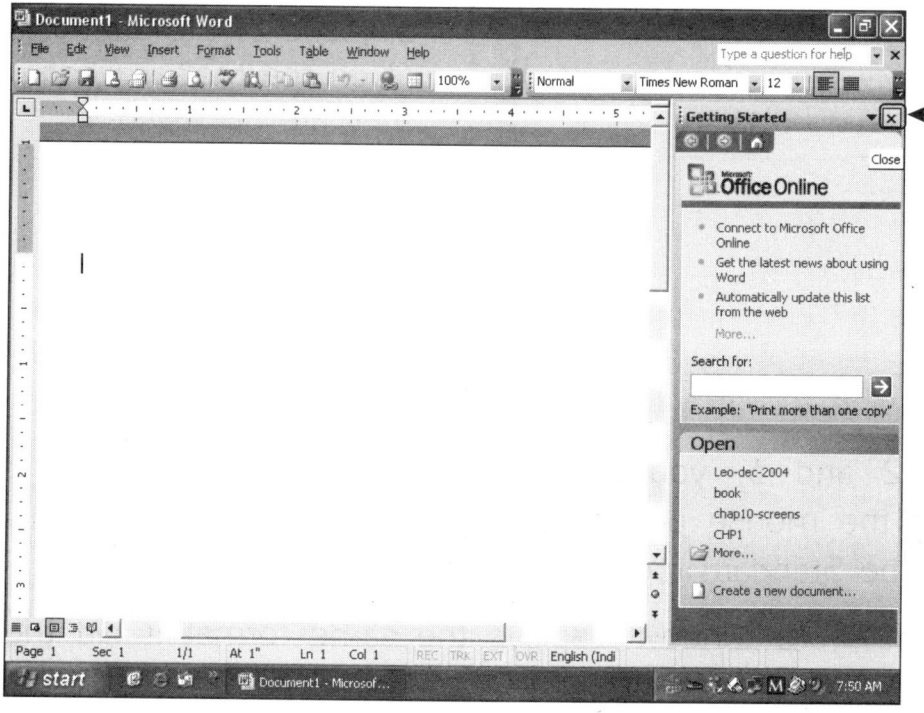

1. Click on the **Close** button in the upper-right corner of the task pane title bar.

Drag and Drop Series

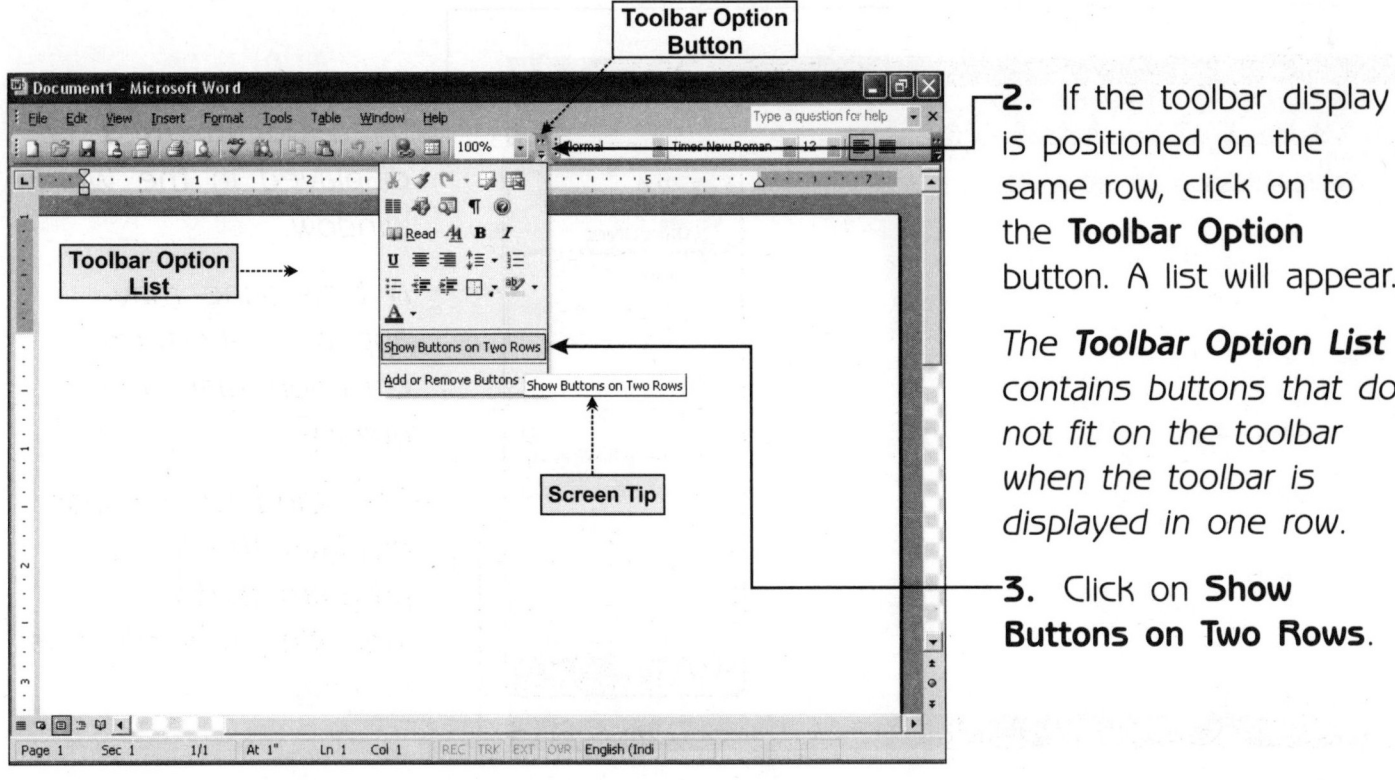

2. If the toolbar display is positioned on the same row, click on to the **Toolbar Option** button. A list will appear.

   *The **Toolbar Option List** contains buttons that do not fit on the toolbar when the toolbar is displayed in one row.*

3. Click on **Show Buttons on Two Rows**.

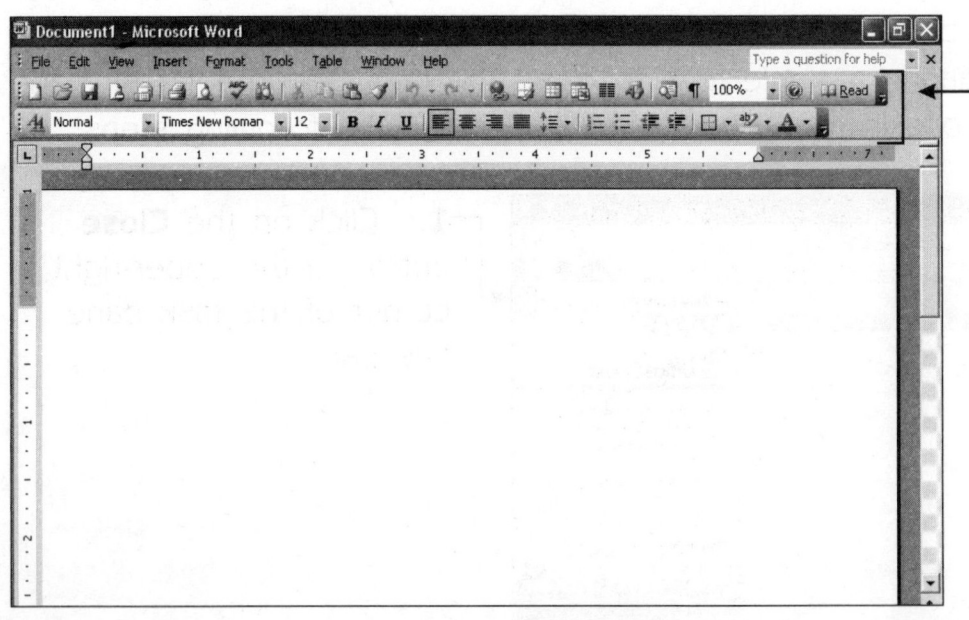

Word displays the toolbars in two separate rows. The Toolbar Option list is empty because all the buttons fit on the toolbar when they are displayed in two rows.

As an alternative to Steps 2 and 3, you can point to the left edge of the Formatting toolbar, and when the mouse pointer changes to a four-headed arrow, drag the toolbar down below the Standard toolbar to create two rows.

Each time you start Word, the Word window displays the same format it did the last time you used Word.

The Word Window

The Word window includes a variety of items that make your work more efficient and documents more professional. They are described in the following sections:

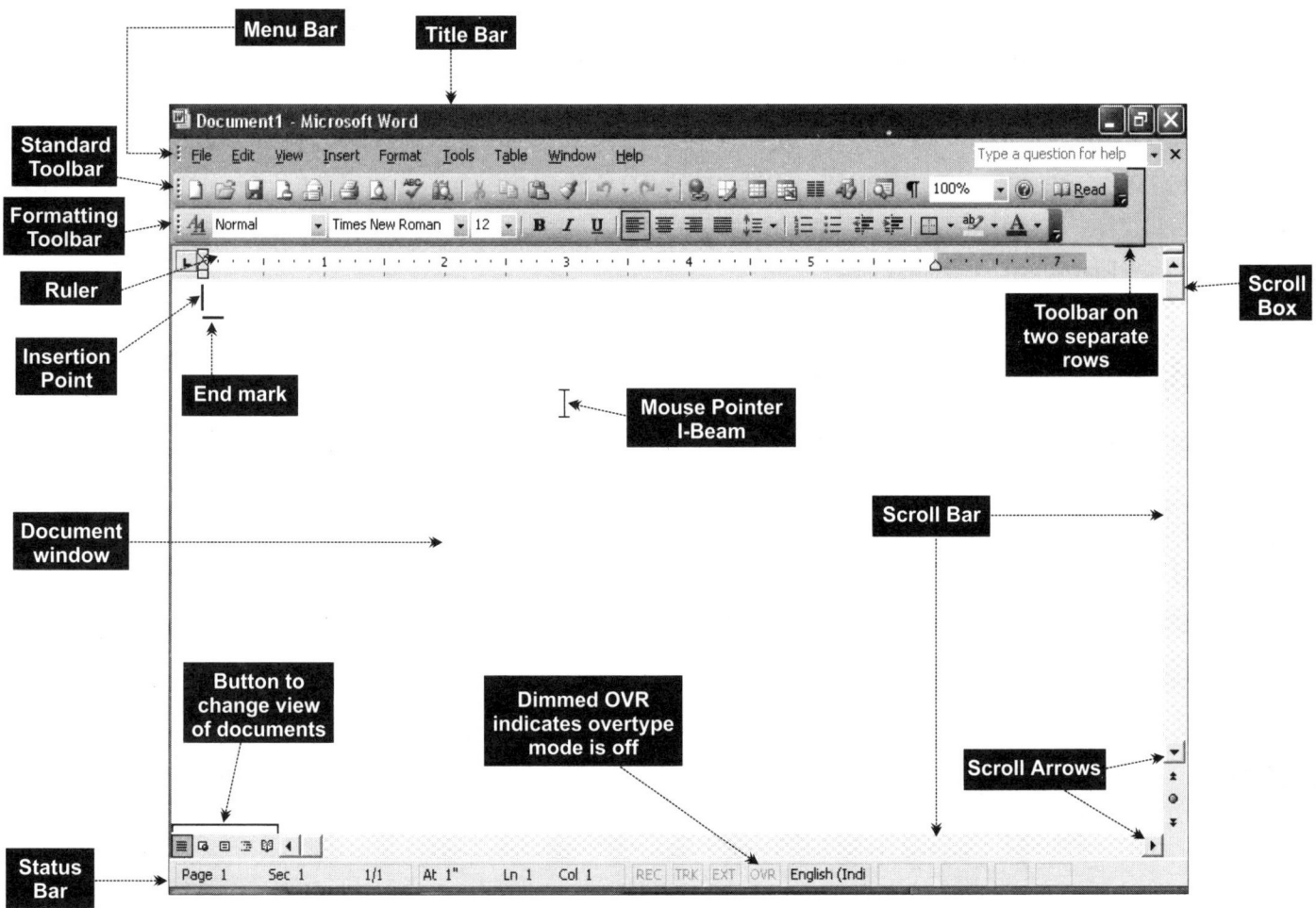

The main elements of the Word document window are the insertion point, end mark, mouse pointer, rulers, scroll bars and status bar, as shown above in the figure. These elements are unique to Word or may be common in other applications. It also displays text, tables, graphics and other items as they are typed or inserted into the document.

A blinking vertical bar that indicates where the text will be inserted as you type is called the **insertion point**. A short horizontal line that indicates the end of your document is the **end mark**.

Drag and Drop Series

The **mouse pointer** changes shape depending on the task you are performing in Word and the pointer's location on the screen. The mouse pointer has the shape of an I-beam on the screen in the previous page. However, the mouse pointer can change to other shapes as well.

You can display different portions of your document in the document window by using the **scroll bars**.

The **status bar** is displayed at the bottom of the document window, above the Windows taskbar. It presents information about the location of the insertion point and the progress of current tasks, as well as the status of certain commands, keys and buttons.

Menu Bar

A special toolbar that displays the Word menu names is the **menu bar**. Each **menu** contains a list of commands, which you can use to perform tasks such as retrieving, storing, printing and formatting data in your document. If you require a particular menu on the menu bar, just click on it. For example, to display the Format menu, click on **Format** on the bar. The menu sometimes, is provided with a submenu that is indicated by an arrow to its right edge.

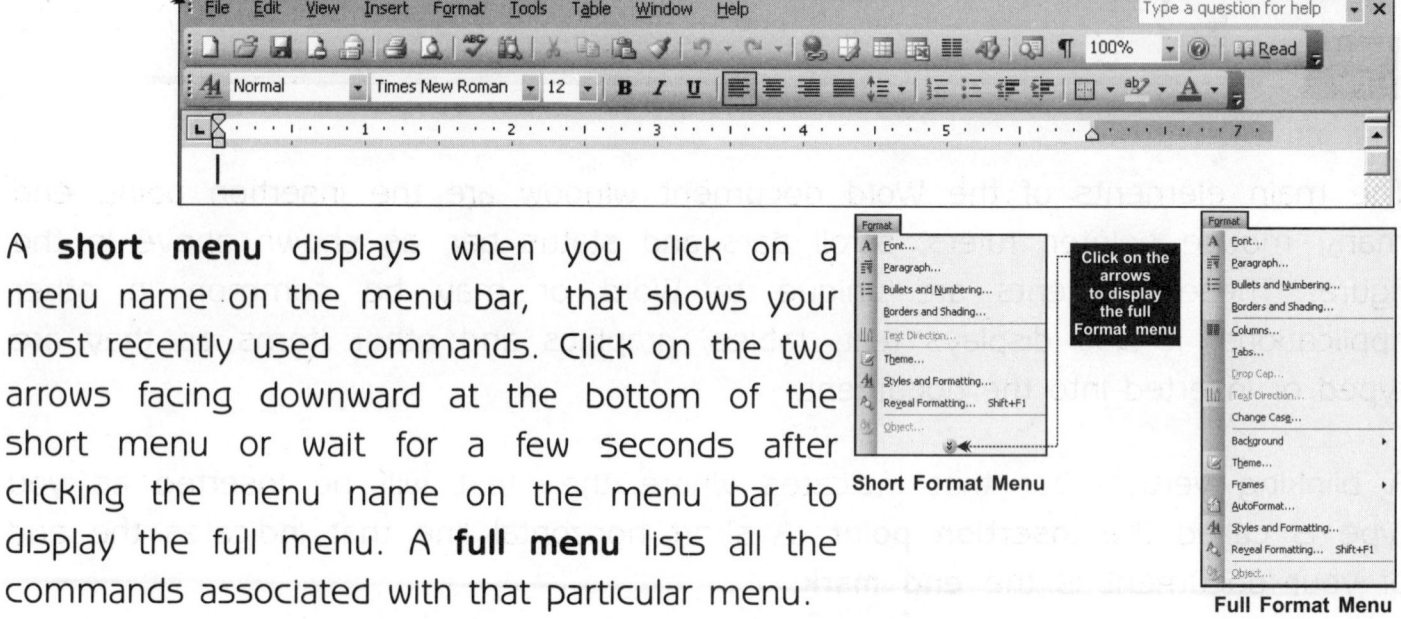

A **short menu** displays when you click on a menu name on the menu bar, that shows your most recently used commands. Click on the two arrows facing downward at the bottom of the short menu or wait for a few seconds after clicking the menu name on the menu bar to display the full menu. A **full menu** lists all the commands associated with that particular menu.

Word

Toolbars

To allow you to perform tasks more quickly than by using the menu bar and related menus, Word has many pre-defined toolbars which contain buttons, boxes and menus. For example, to print a document, you can click on the **Print** button on the toolbar. Each button on the toolbar displays an image to help you remember its function. The two built-in toolbars are **Standard toolbar** and **Formatting toolbar**. The Standard toolbar, with its buttons and boxes, is illustrated in **figure 1**. The Formatting toolbar is illustrated in **figure 2**. Each button and box is described in a detailed manner subsequently as they are used.

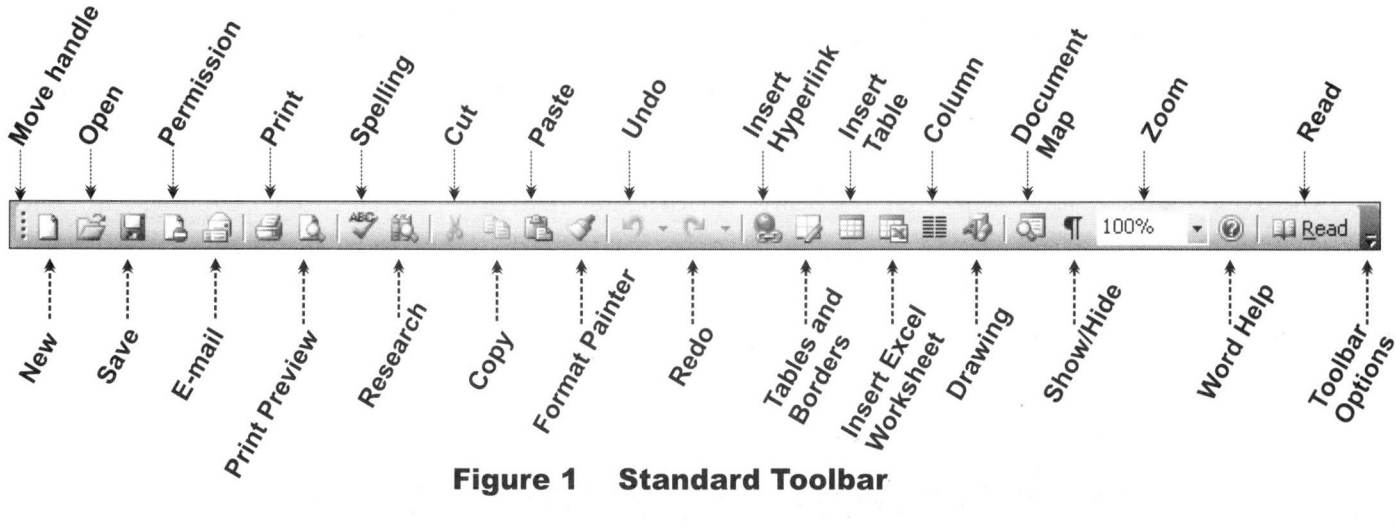

Figure 1   Standard Toolbar

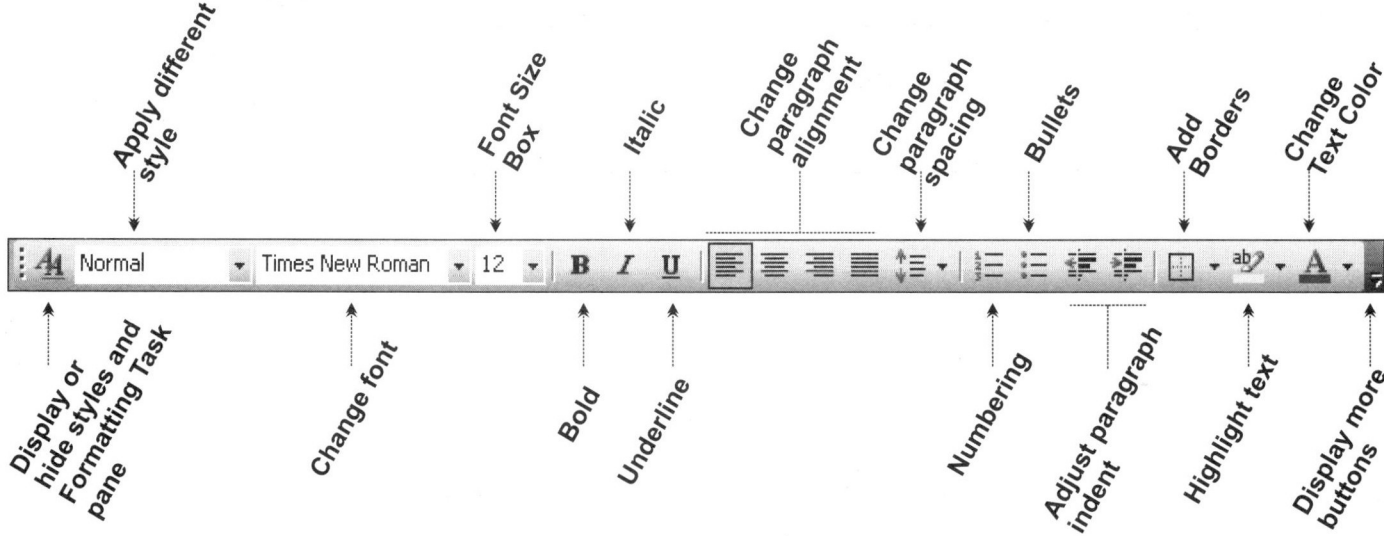

Figure 2   Formatting Toolbar

11

2. Creating Documents

Changing Default Font Size

The characters that are displayed on the screen have a specific shape, size and style. The font or typeface defines appearance and shape of the letters, numbers and special characters. **Times New Roman** is the preset or default font used in Word. **Font size**, which is determined by a measurement system called **points**, specifies the size of the characters. About 1/72 of one inch in height is a single **point**. Thus, a character with a font size of 12 is about 12/72 or 1/6 of one inch in height. 12 is the most commonly used default font size in Word.

The default font size can be easily changed before you start typing if the characters in your document require larger font size than the default.

To Change the Font Size

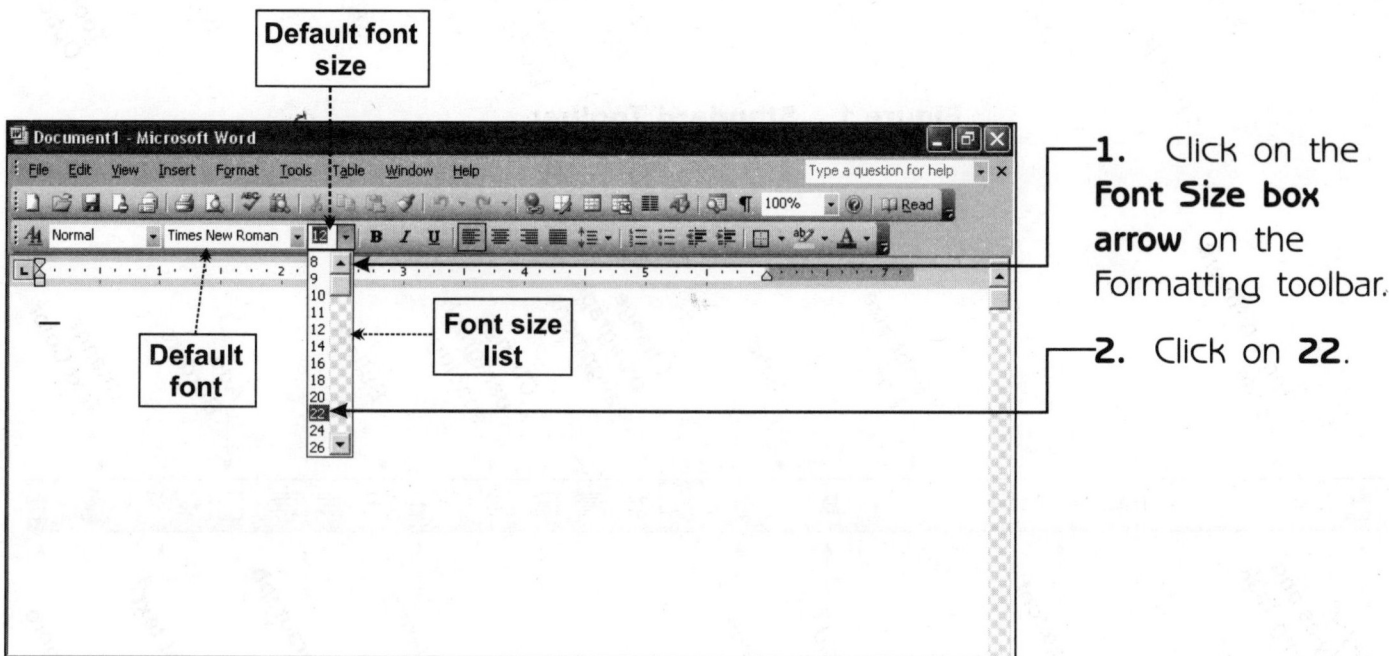

1. Click on the **Font Size box arrow** on the Formatting toolbar.

2. Click on **22**.

A list of available font size is displayed in the **Font size list**. The available font size depends on the current font, which is Times New Roman.

Word

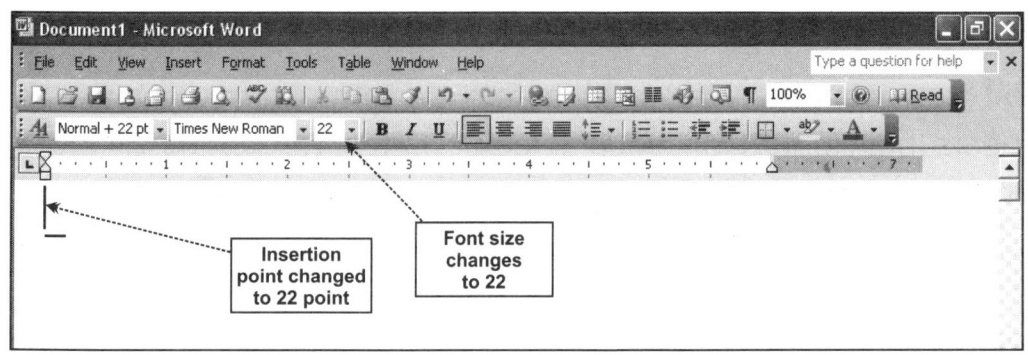

The new font size takes effect immediately in your document. Word uses this font size for characters you type into this document.

The font size for characters entered in this document changes to 22. The size of the insertion point increases to reflect the new font size.

Entering Text in Word

Word processors have brought about a significant change in the way the text is typed in a document. The insertion point is automatically transferred to the next line, once you reach the end of your previous line in the same paragraph in Word. Hence, you do not need to press any other key except the enter key while beginning to type in a new paragraph in your document or if wish to leave a blank line. Your typed in text will appear where the insertion point flashes on your screen.

Type the text for your document.

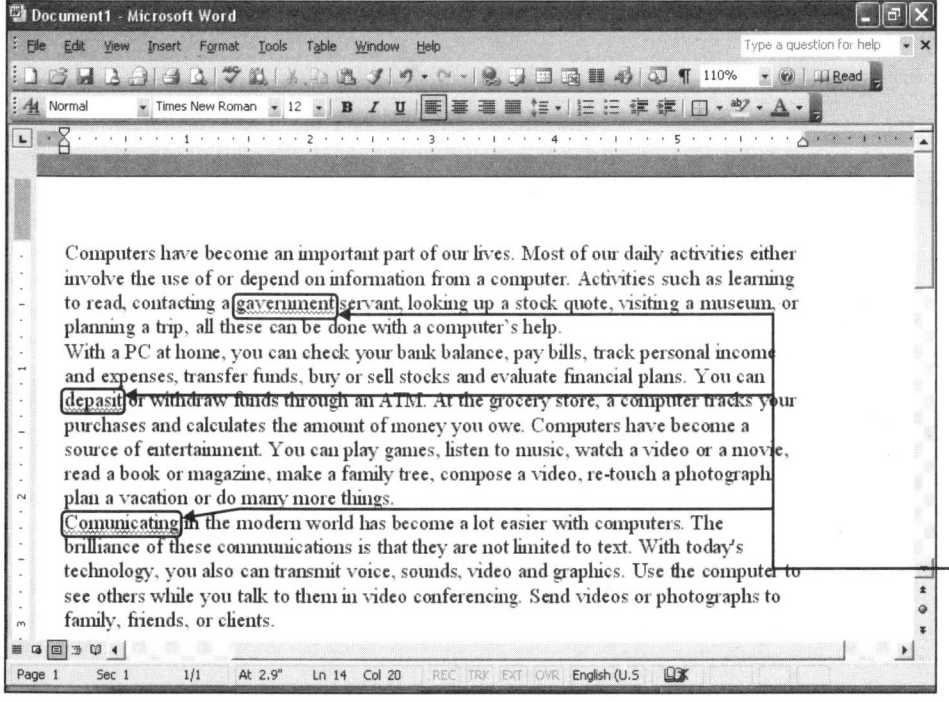

When you reach the end of a line, Word automatically wraps the text to the next line. You only need to press the **Enter** key when you want to start a new paragraph.

Word automatically underlines misspelled words in red and grammar errors in green. The underlines will not appear when you print your document.

Drag and Drop Series

Selecting Text

You must select the text you want to work with before performing many tasks in Word. Selected text appears highlighted on your screen. There are several different ways to select words and paragraphs. One way is by holding down the left button of the mouse and dragging the cursor till the end of the required text. The other way is to use double-click and triple-click combinations of the mouse button to select whole words or paragraphs.

To Select a Word

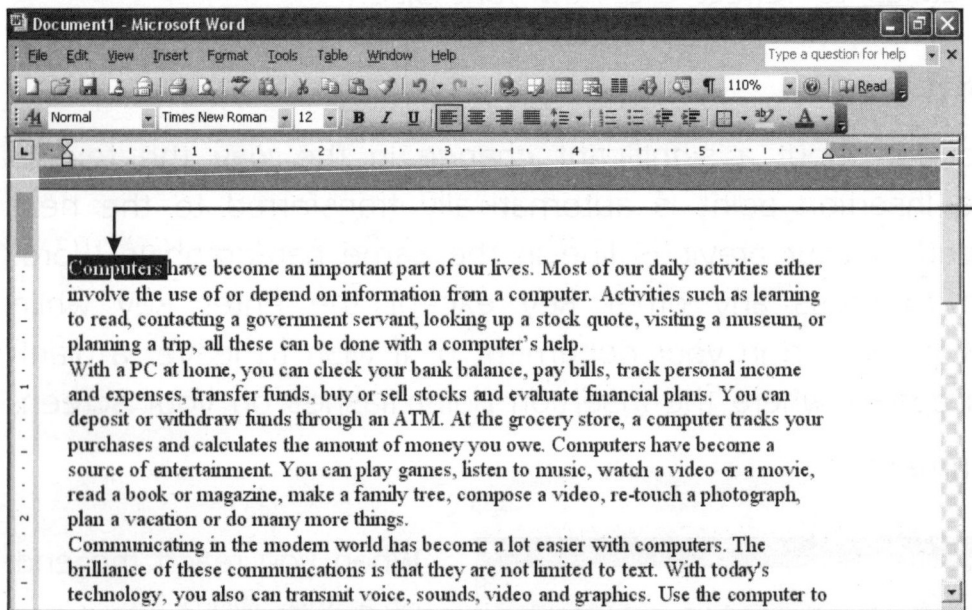

1. Double-click on the word you want to select.

2. To deselect the word, click outside the selected area.

To Select a Sentence

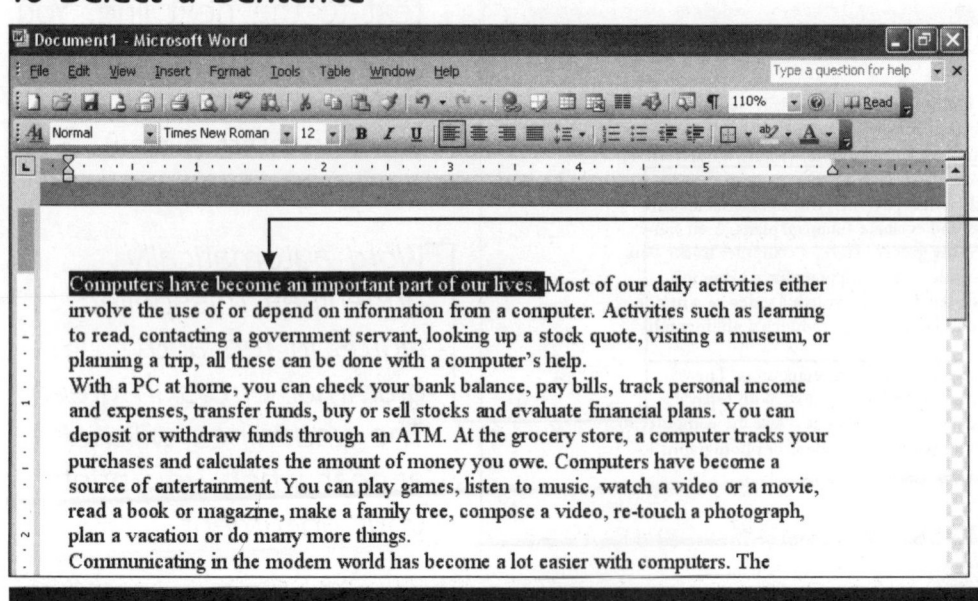

1. Press and hold down the **Ctrl** key.

2. Still holding down the **Ctrl** key, click on the sentence you want to select.

14

To Select a Paragraph

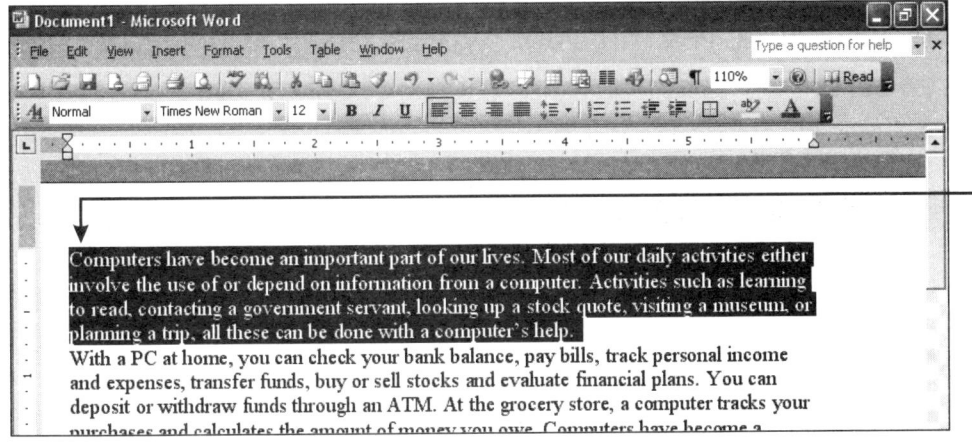

1. Place the mouse pointer (I) over the paragraph you want to select and then quickly click three times (triple-click).

To Select Any Amount of Text

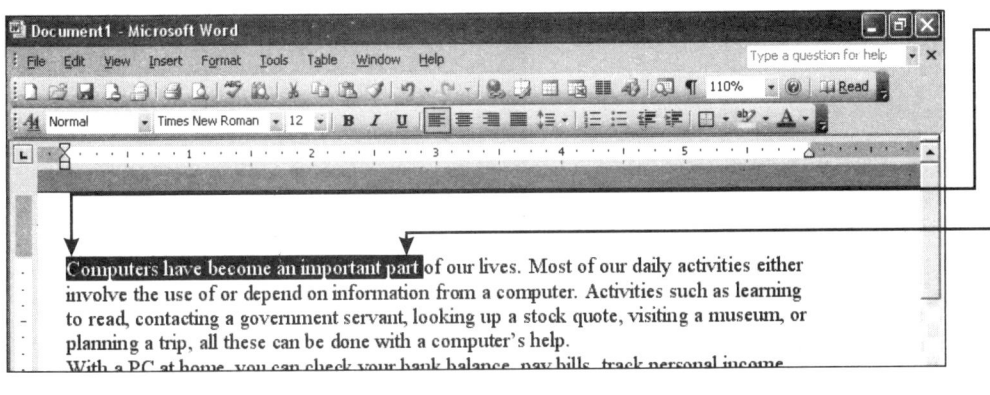

1. Place the mouse pointer (I) over the first word you want to select.

2. Drag the mouse pointer (I) over the text you want to select.

Moving in a Document

Moving to another location in the document is done in the following ways:

To Move the Insertion Point

The insertion point is a flashing line on your screen which indicates where the text you type will appear. So click where you want to place the insertion point.

To Use the Scroll Bar

To scroll up, down, right or left, you can use the scroll bar by dragging the scroll box along the scroll bar. You can also use the scroll arrows for moving in the document.

The location of the scroll box indicates which part of the document you are viewing. To view the middle of the document, drag the scroll box halfway down the scroll bar.

Drag and Drop Series

Zooming In or Out

You can enlarge or reduce the display of text on your screen. You can increase the zoom setting to view an area of your document in more detail or decrease the zoom setting to view more of your document at once.

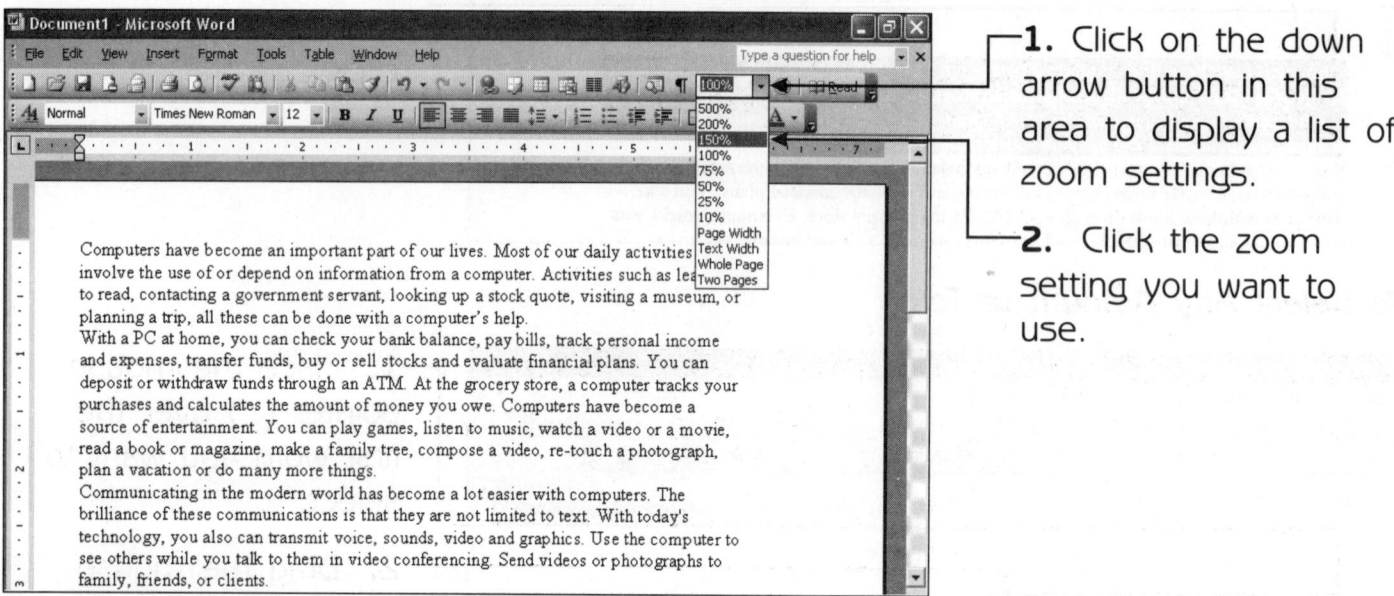

1. Click on the down arrow button in this area to display a list of zoom settings.

2. Click the zoom setting you want to use.

Select **Page Width** or **Text Width** to fit the page or the text across the width of your screen. Select **Whole Page** or **Two Pages** to display one or two full pages across your screen.

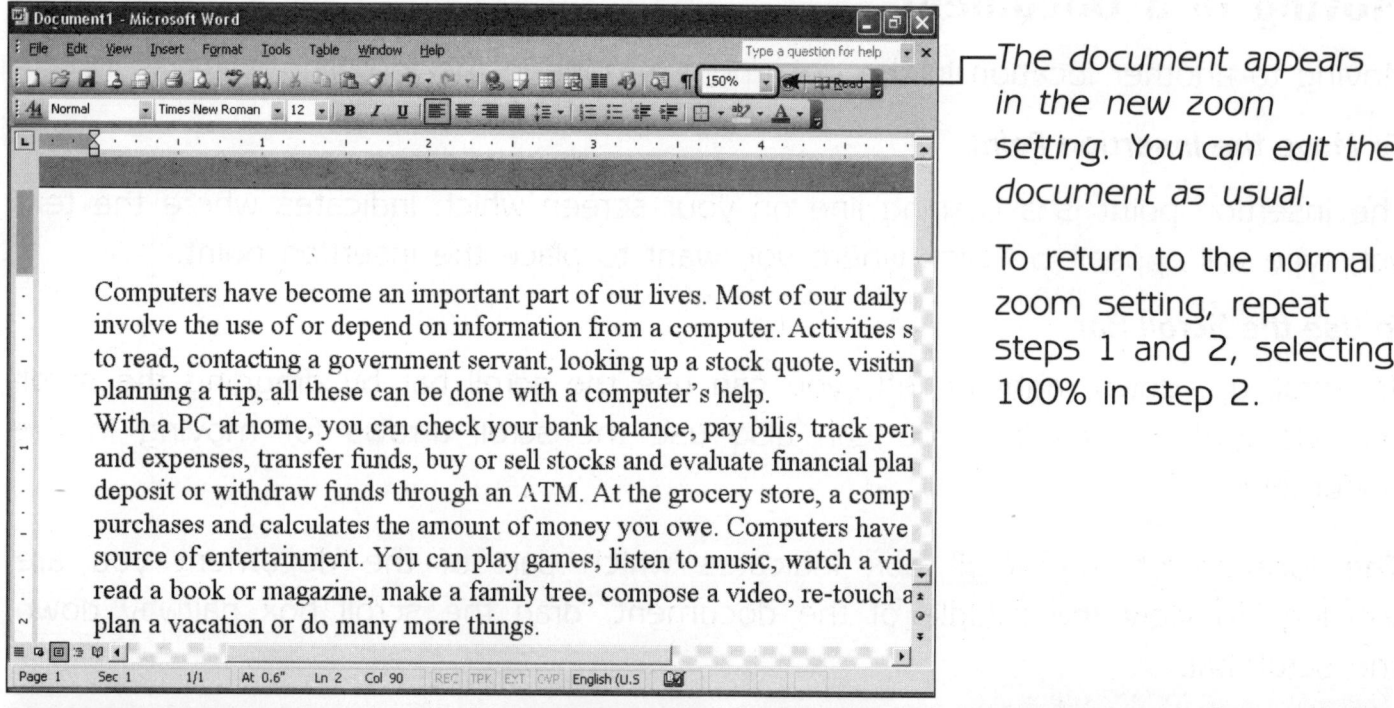

The document appears in the new zoom setting. You can edit the document as usual.

To return to the normal zoom setting, repeat steps 1 and 2, selecting 100% in step 2.

Word

Saving a Document

You can save your document to store it for future use. Saving a document allows you to review and edit it later. This saved file can be used on other computers. One handy tool that the Word program uses is a **dialog box** that reminds you to save your work before closing a program. This ensures that your valuable work is not lost simply because you clicked the Close button (x) when you did not really mean to.

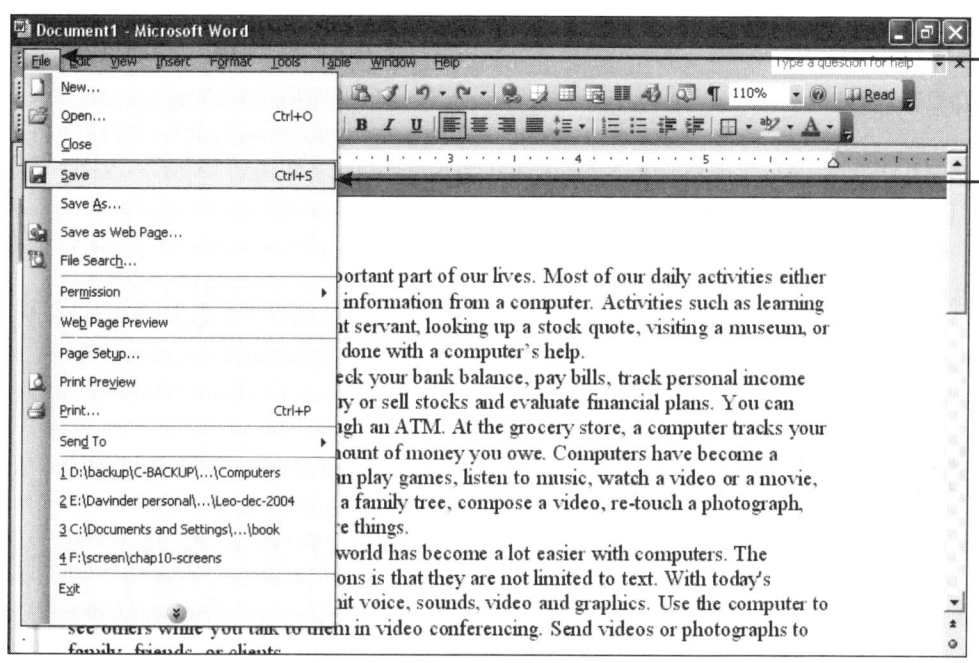

1. Click on **File**. The File menu will appear.

2. Click on **Save** in the File menu.

The **Save As** dialog box will appear.

*If you have previously saved your document, the **Save As** dialog box will not appear since you have already named the document.*

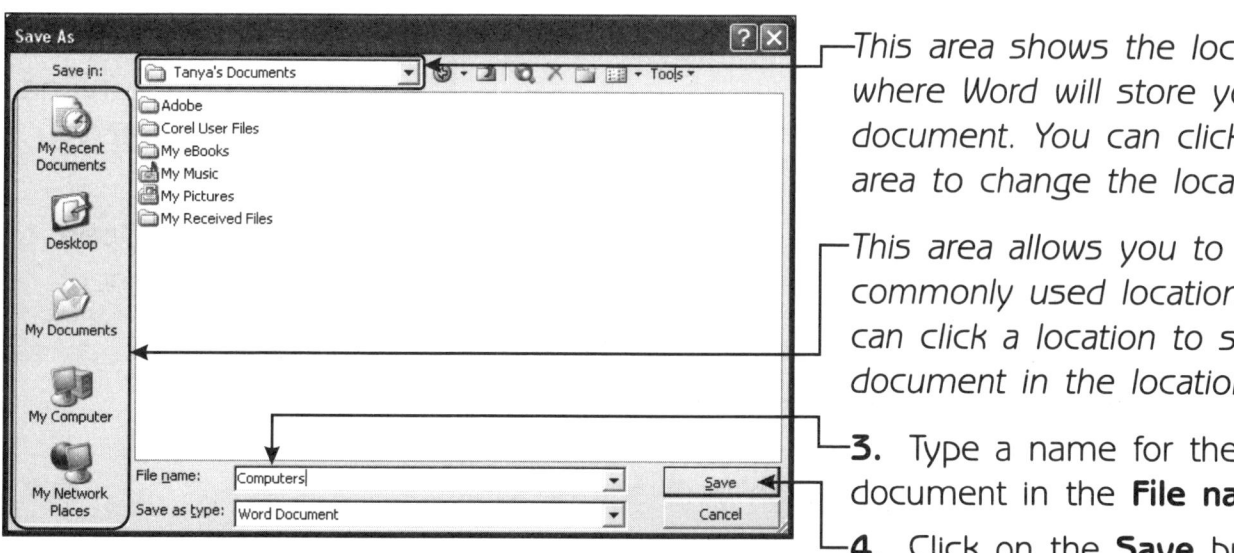

This area shows the location where Word will store your document. You can click this area to change the location.

This area allows you to access commonly used locations. You can click a location to save your document in the location.

3. Type a name for the document in the **File name:** box.

4. Click on the **Save** button to save the document.

17

Drag and Drop Series

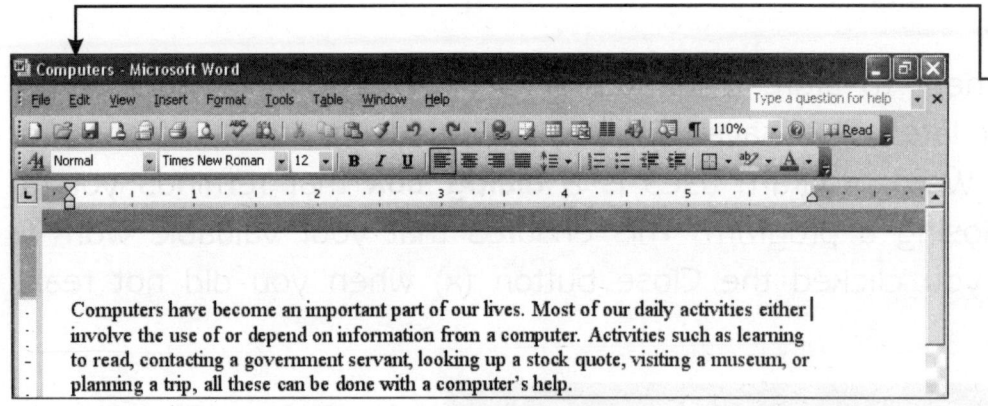

Word saves your document and displays the name of the document at the top of your screen.

Opening a Saved Document

You can open a saved document to view it on your screen. This allows you to review and make changes in the document.

1. Click on the **Open** button (📂) on the standard toolbar to open a document. The **Open** dialog box appears.

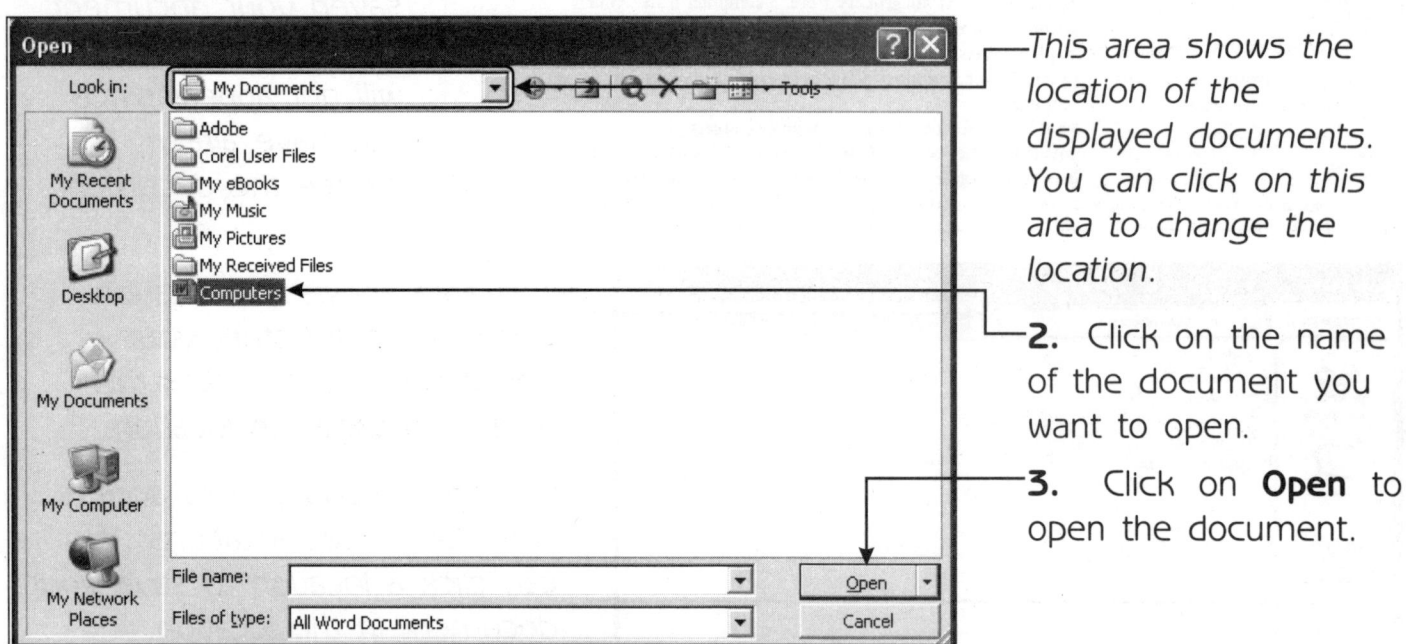

This area shows the location of the displayed documents. You can click on this area to change the location.

2. Click on the name of the document you want to open.

3. Click on **Open** to open the document.

The document will open and appear on your screen.

The title bar will display the name of the open document.

3. Editing the Text

Inserting Text in a Document

You can easily add new text or insert text in your current document.

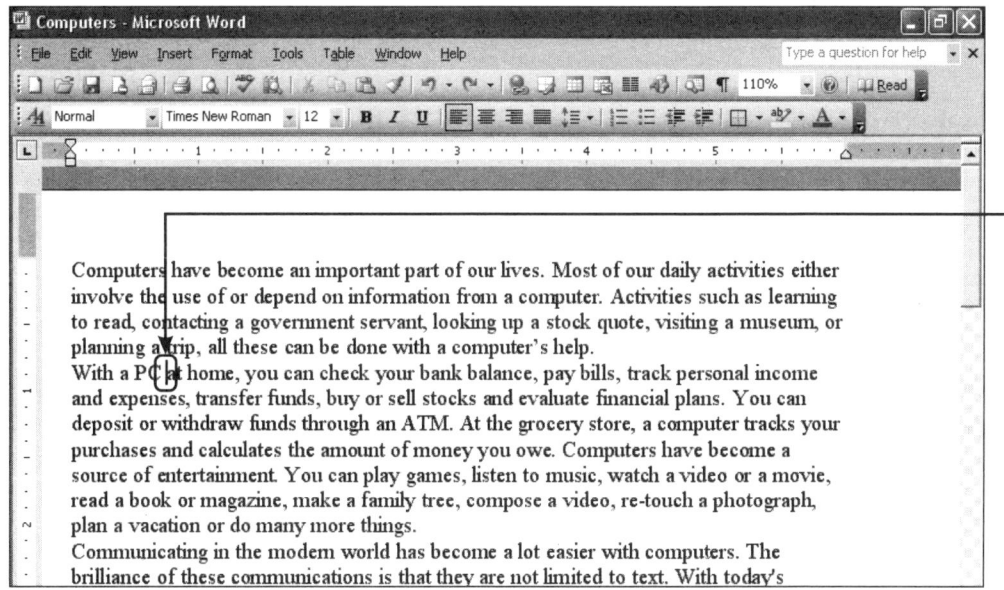

1. Click on the location in your document where you want to insert the new text.

   The text you type will appear where the insertion point flashes on the screen.

You can press the arrow keys on the keyboard to move the insertion point one character or line in any direction.

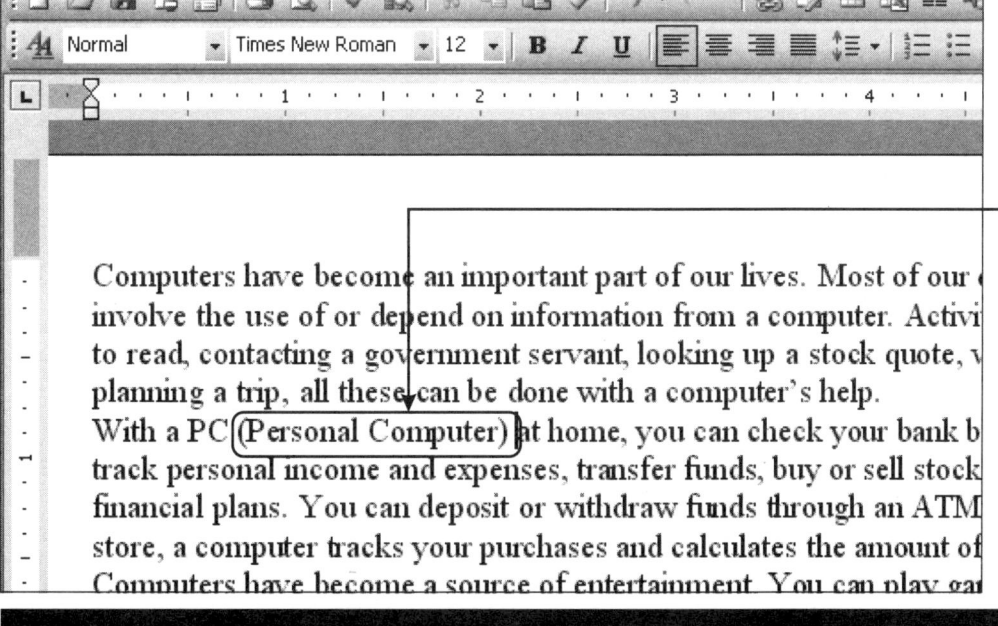

2. Type the text you want to insert. To insert a blank space, press the **Spacebar** on the keyboard.

   The words to the right of the new text move forward.

Drag and Drop Series

Deleting Text in a Document

To remove text from the document you no longer need, perform the following steps:

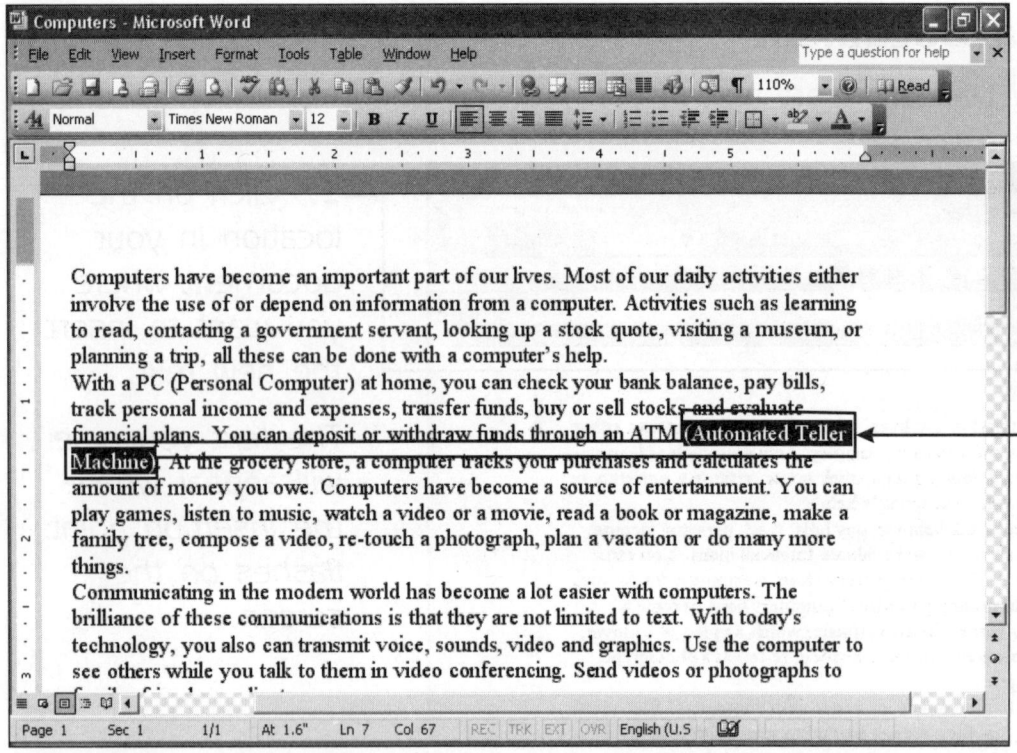

1. Select the text you want to delete.

2. Press the **Delete** key on the keyboard to remove the text.

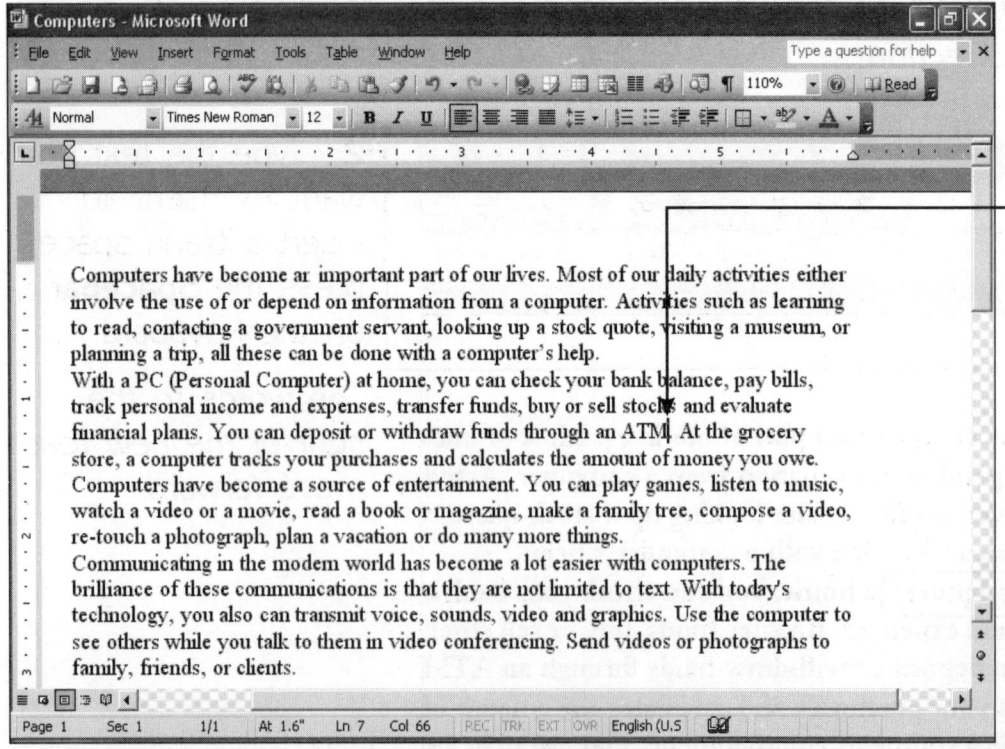

The text disappears. The remaining text in the line or paragraph moves to fill the empty space.

20

Word

Moving and Copying Text

You can move or copy text to a new location in your document. Moving or copying text allows you to rearrange or repeat text in your document. When you move text, the text disappears from its original location. When you copy text, the text appears in both the original and new locations.

To Use Drag and Drop

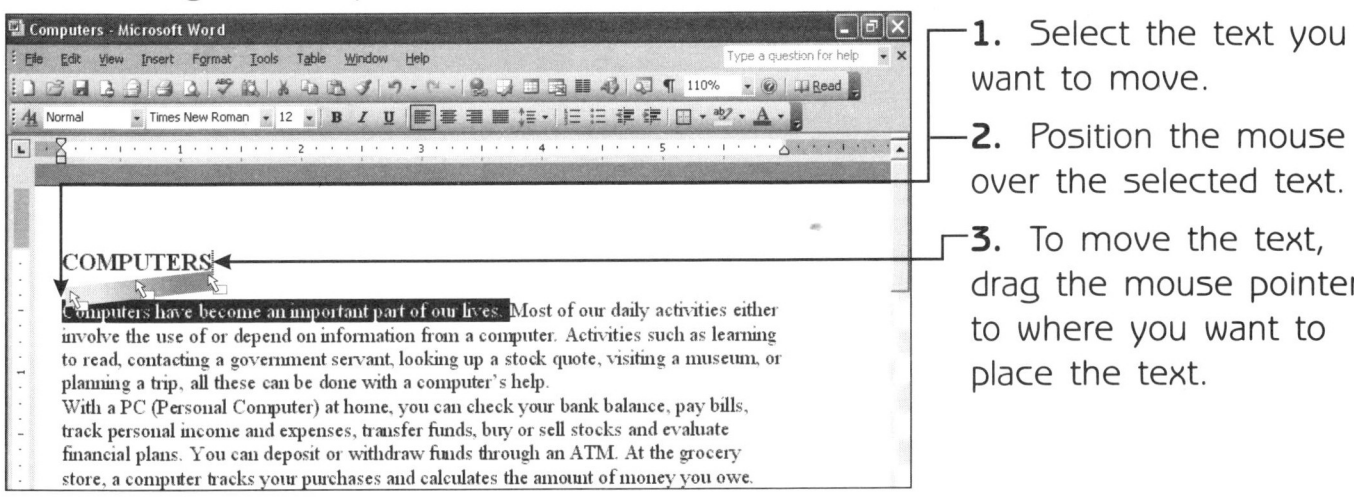

1. Select the text you want to move.
2. Position the mouse over the selected text.
3. To move the text, drag the mouse pointer to where you want to place the text.

The text will appear where you position the dotted insertion point on your screen.

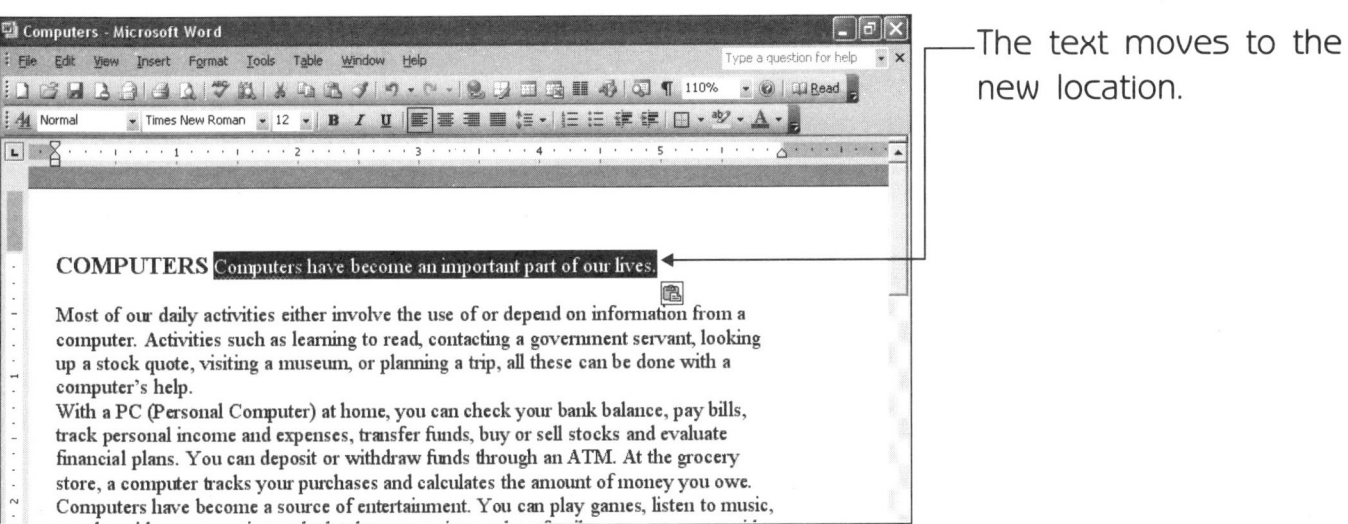

The text moves to the new location.

To copy text, perform steps **1** to **3**. Press and hold down the **Ctrl** key as you perform step **3**.

Drag and Drop Series

To Use the Toolbar Buttons

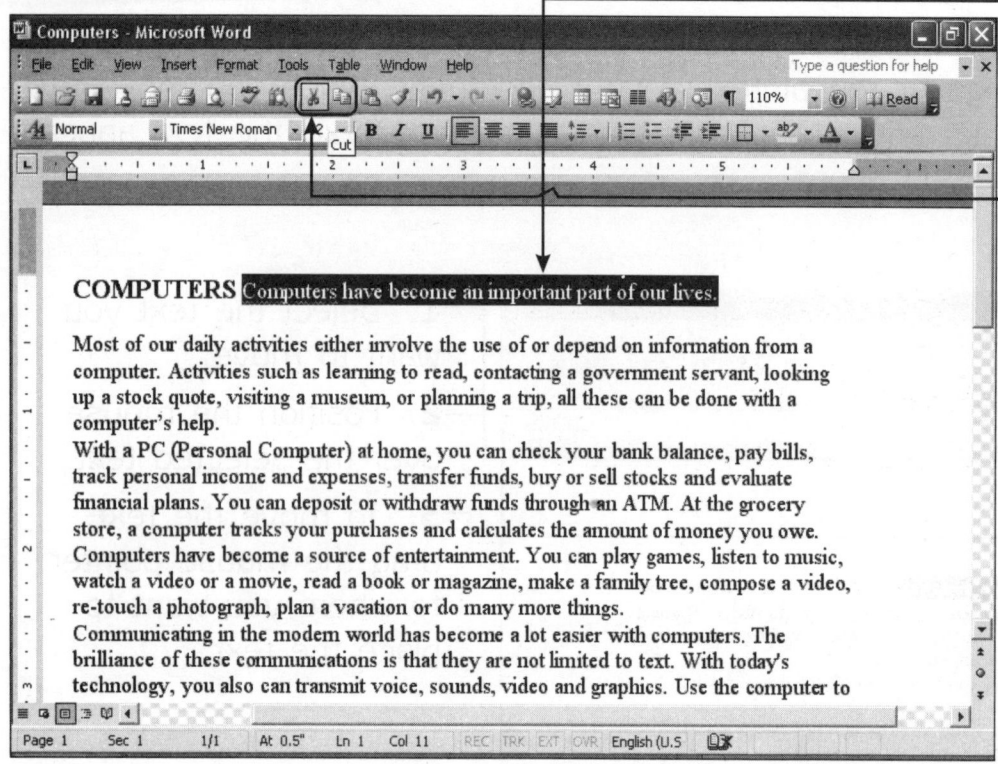

1. Select the text you want to move or copy.

2. Click one of the following buttons:

   Cut text (✂)

   Copy text (📋)

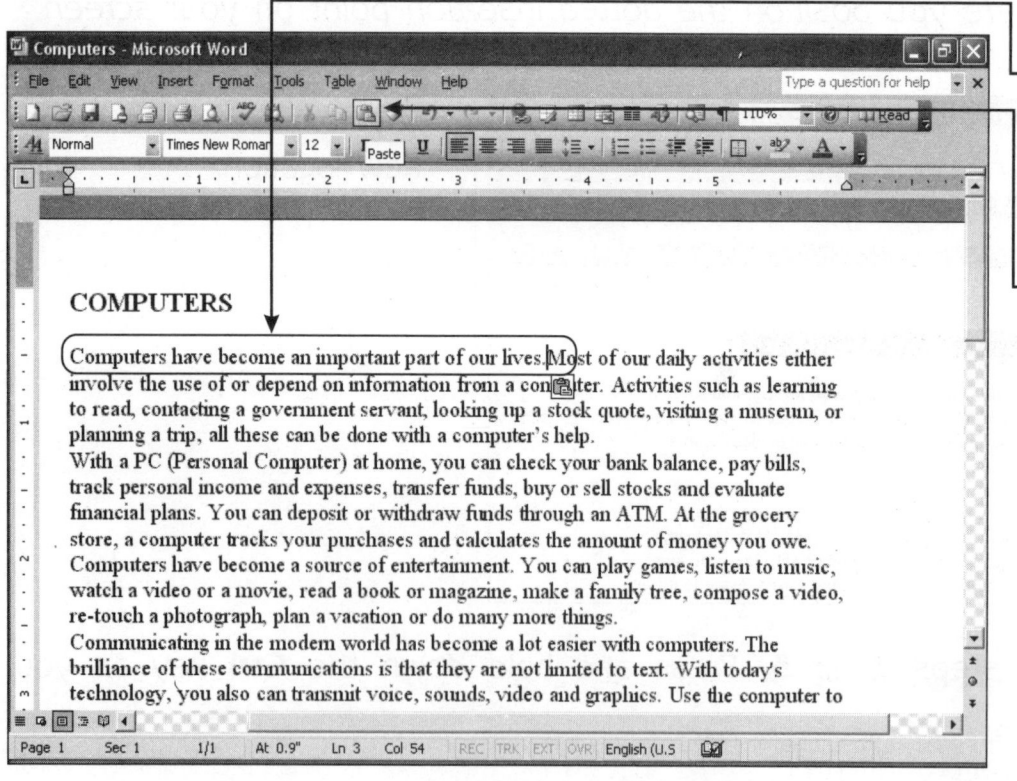

3. Click on the location where you want to place the text.

4. Click on the **Paste** button (📋) on the Standard toolbar to place the text in the new location.

The text appears in the new location.

22

Word

Inserting the Date and Time

Date and Time can be inserted into your document. Word can automatically update the date and time each time you open or print the document. Word uses the date and time of your computer's built-in clock.

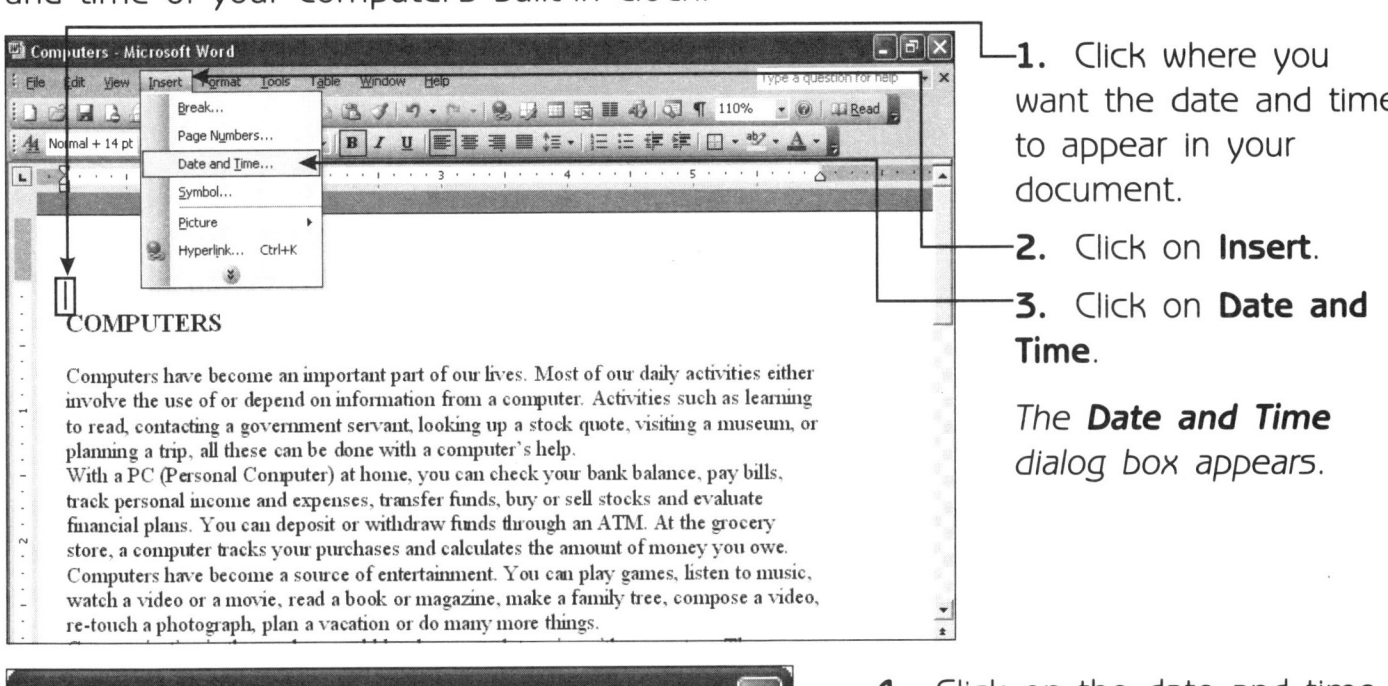

1. Click where you want the date and time to appear in your document.

2. Click on **Insert**.

3. Click on **Date and Time**.

*The **Date and Time** dialog box appears.*

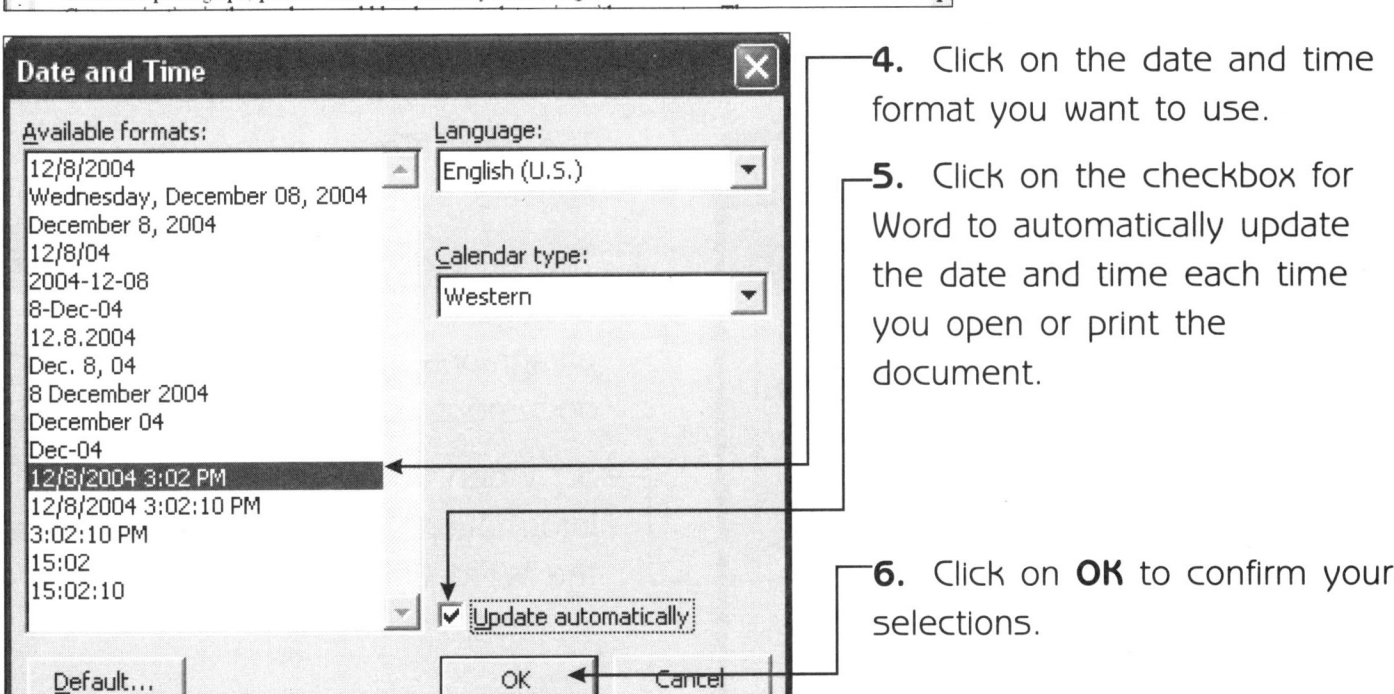

4. Click on the date and time format you want to use.

5. Click on the checkbox for Word to automatically update the date and time each time you open or print the document.

6. Click on **OK** to confirm your selections.

The date and time format you selected appears in your document.

Drag and Drop Series

Counting Words in a Document

Word Count feature can count the number of words in your document.

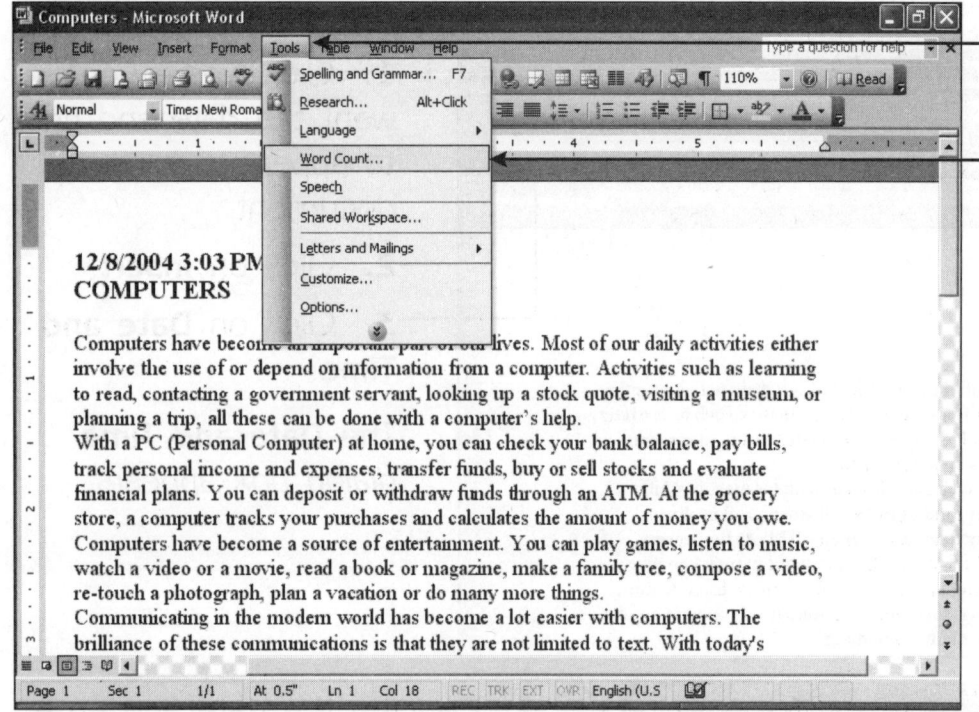

1. Click on **Tools**. The Tools menu will appear.

2. Click on **Word Count**.

To count the number of words in only a part of your document, select the text before performing step 1.

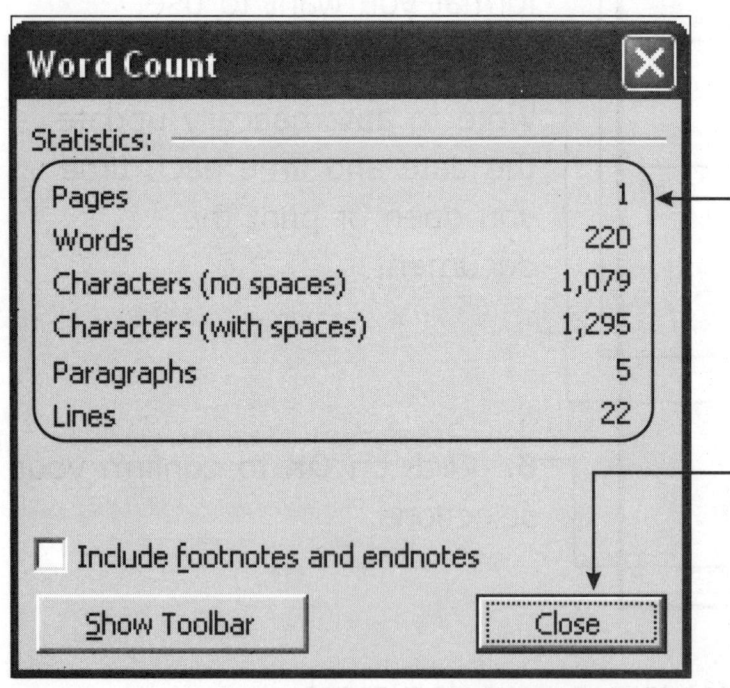

The **Word Count** dialog box appears.

This area displays the total number of pages, words, characters, paragraphs and lines in your document.

3. When you finish reviewing the information, click on **Close** to close the Word Count dialog box.

Finding and Replacing Text

You can find and replace every occurrence of a word or phrase in your document. This is useful if you have frequently misspelled a name.

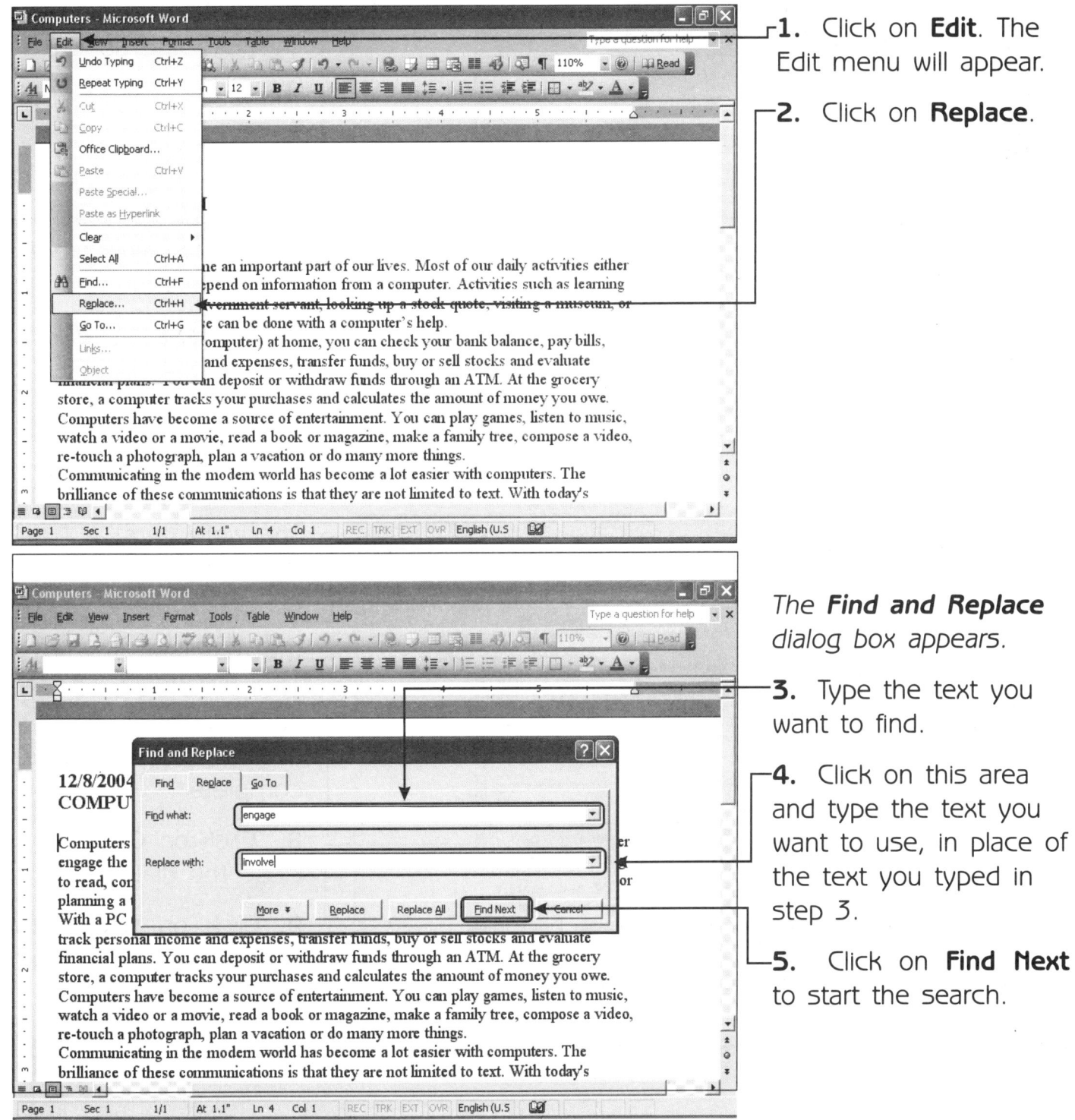

1. Click on **Edit**. The Edit menu will appear.

2. Click on **Replace**.

*The **Find and Replace** dialog box appears.*

3. Type the text you want to find.

4. Click on this area and type the text you want to use, in place of the text you typed in step 3.

5. Click on **Find Next** to start the search.

Drag and Drop Series

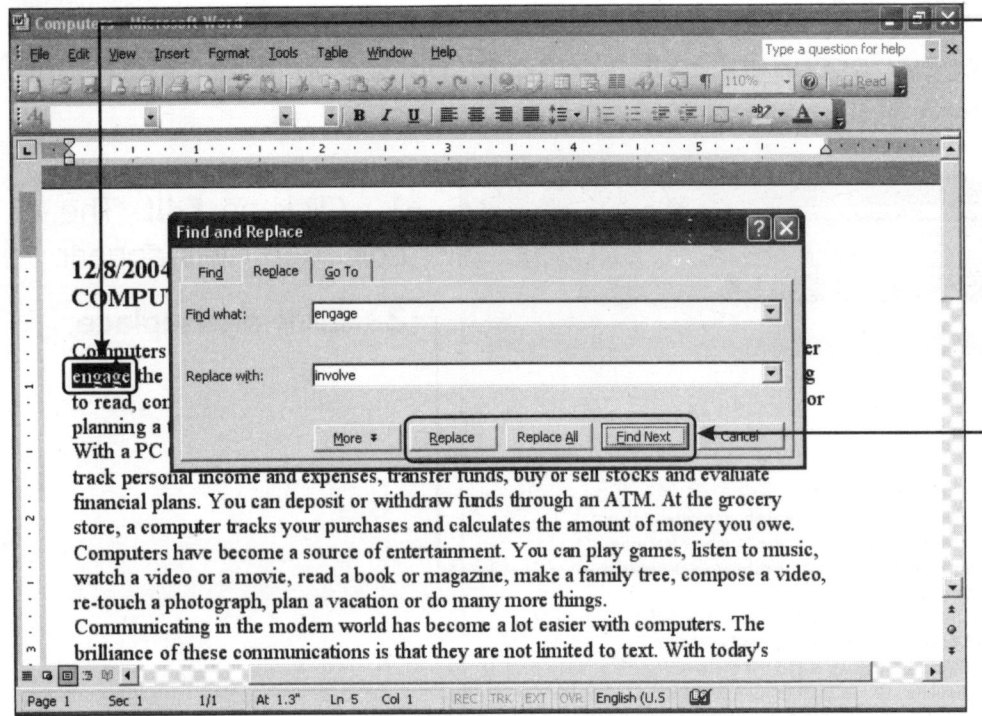

Word highlights the first matching word it finds.

6. Click on one of the following options:

Replace - *Replace the word.*

Replace All - *Replace the word and all the other matching words in the document.*

Find Next - *Ignore the word.*

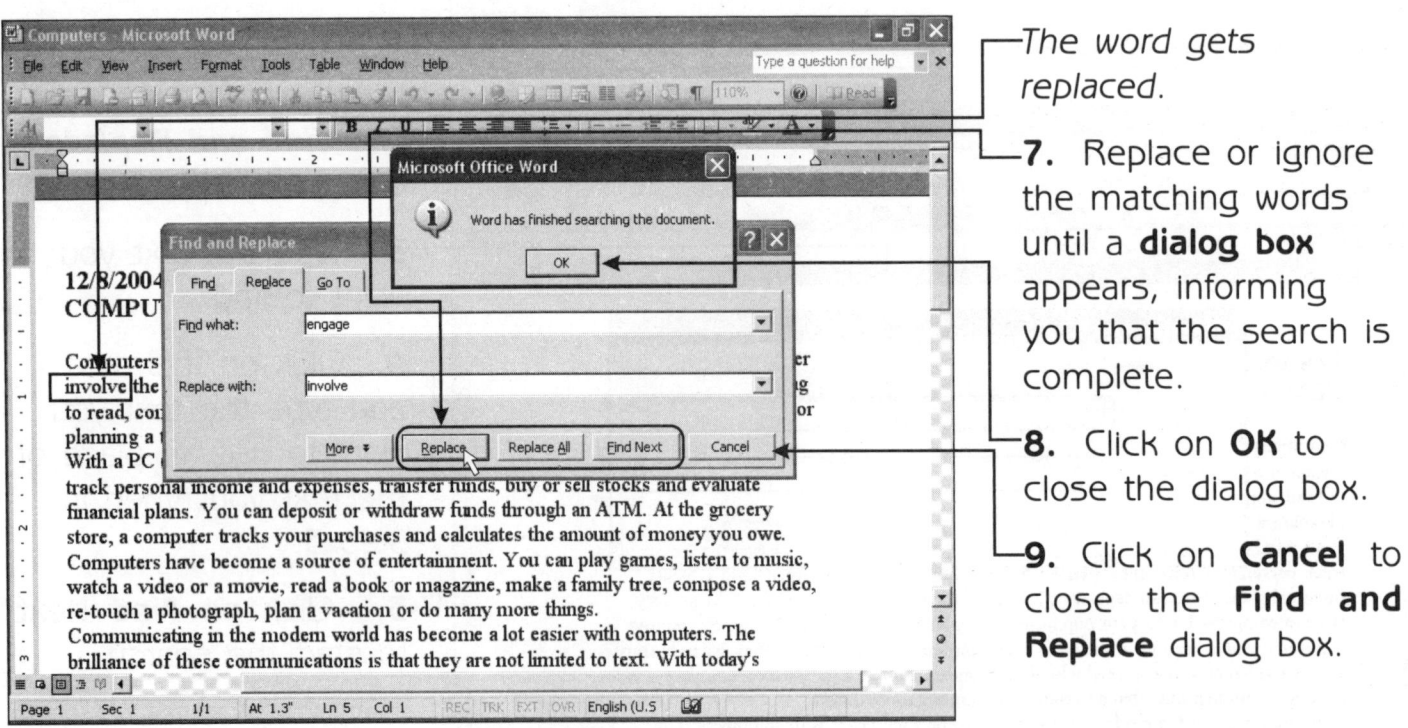

The word gets replaced.

7. Replace or ignore the matching words until a **dialog box** appears, informing you that the search is complete.

8. Click on **OK** to close the dialog box.

9. Click on **Cancel** to close the **Find and Replace** dialog box.

Word

Checking Spelling Mistakes

You can also find and correct spelling errors in your document. MS Word compares every word in your document to words in its dictionary. If a word does not exist in the dictionary, the word is considered misspelled and marked with a red wavy line.

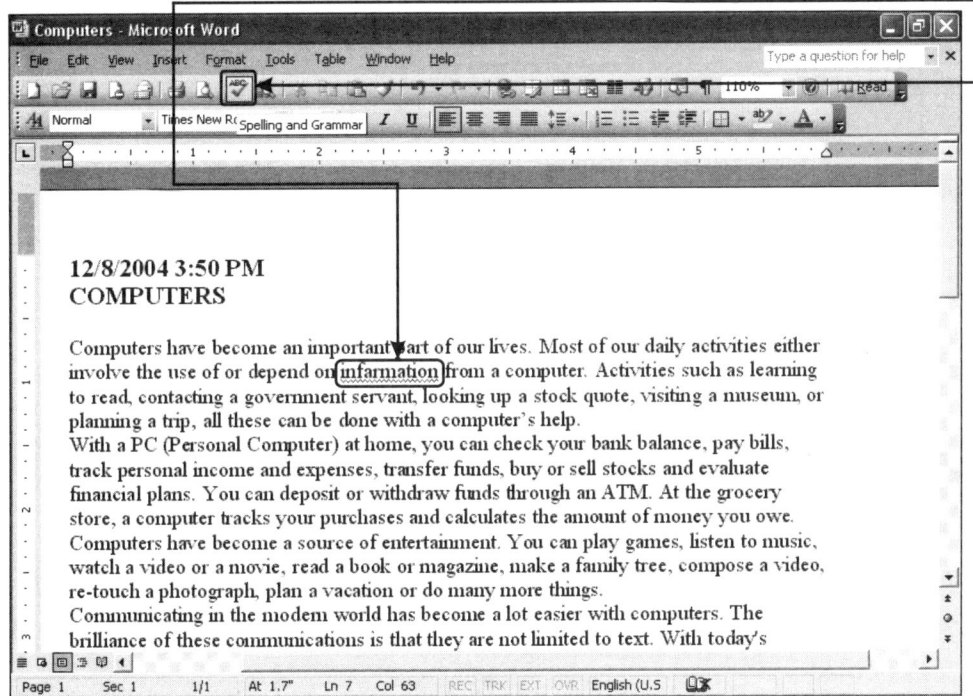

Word automatically underlines misspelled words in red.

1. Click on the **Spelling and Grammar** [🔤] button to start checking your document for spelling and grammatical errors.

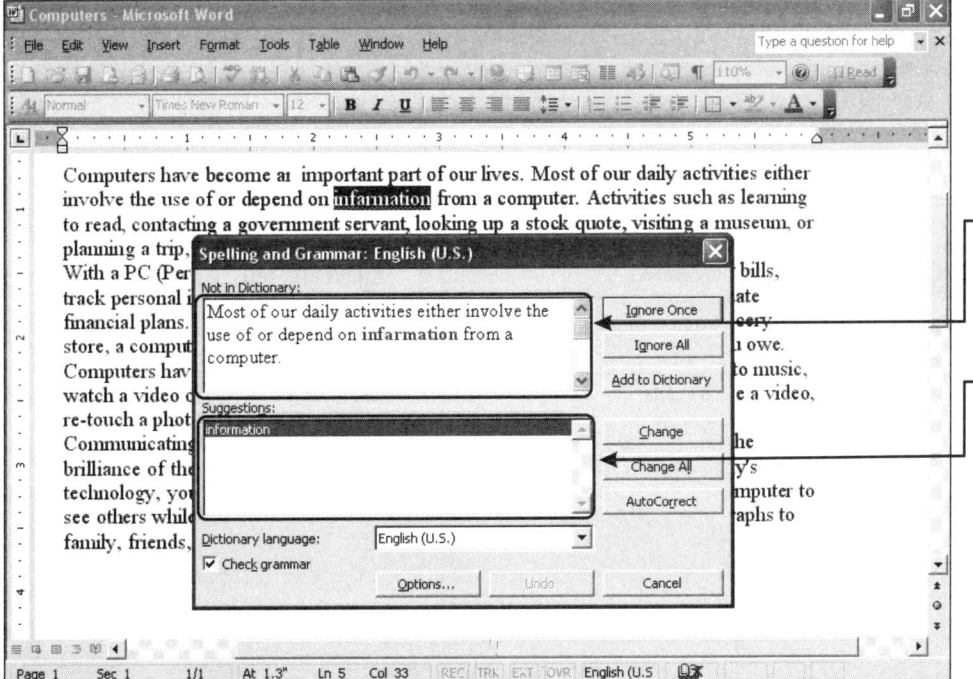

The **Spelling and Grammar** dialog box appears if Word finds an error in your document.

This area displays the first misspelled word or grammatical error.

This area displays suggestions for correcting the error.

27

Drag and Drop Series

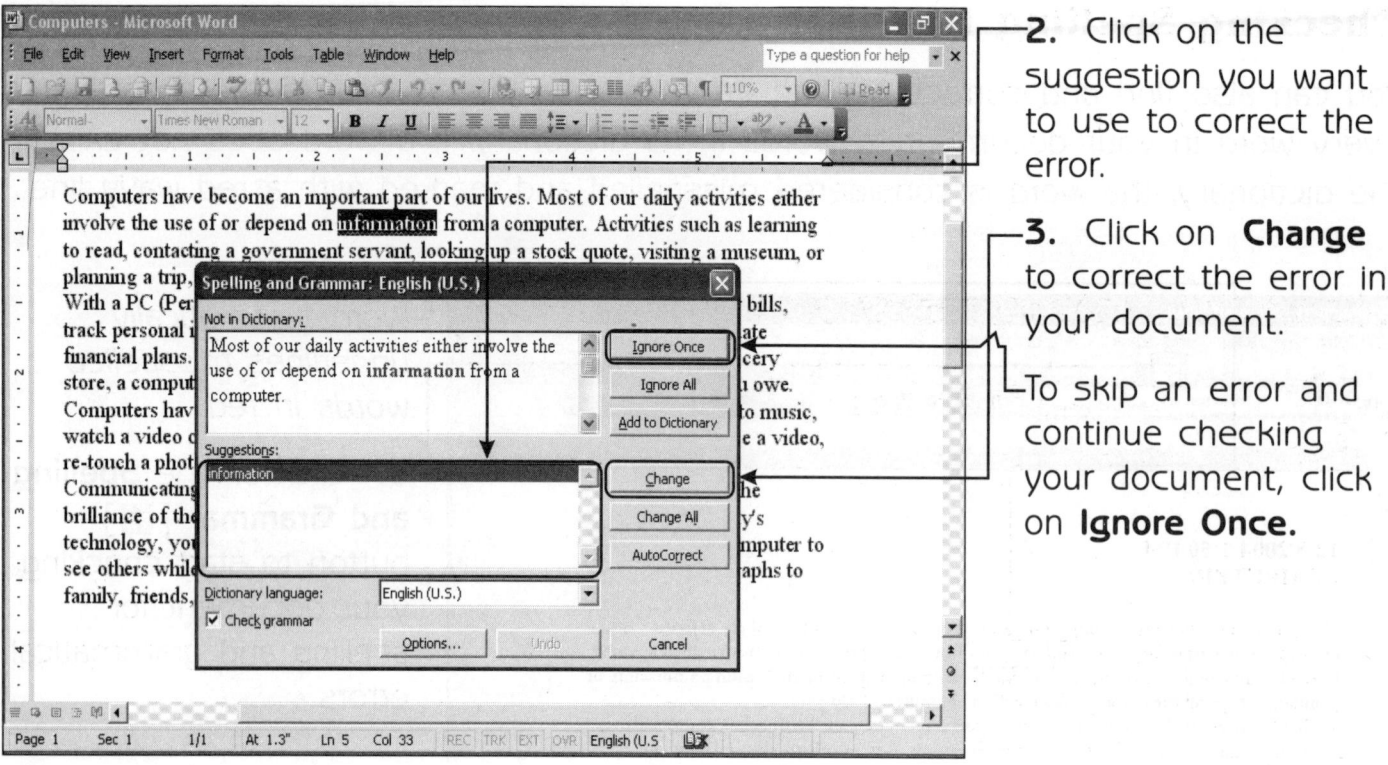

2. Click on the suggestion you want to use to correct the error.

3. Click on **Change** to correct the error in your document.

To skip an error and continue checking your document, click on **Ignore Once.**

To skip an error and all other occurrences of an error in your document, click on **Ignore All** or **Ignore Rule**. The name of the button depends on whether an error is a misspelled word or a grammar error.

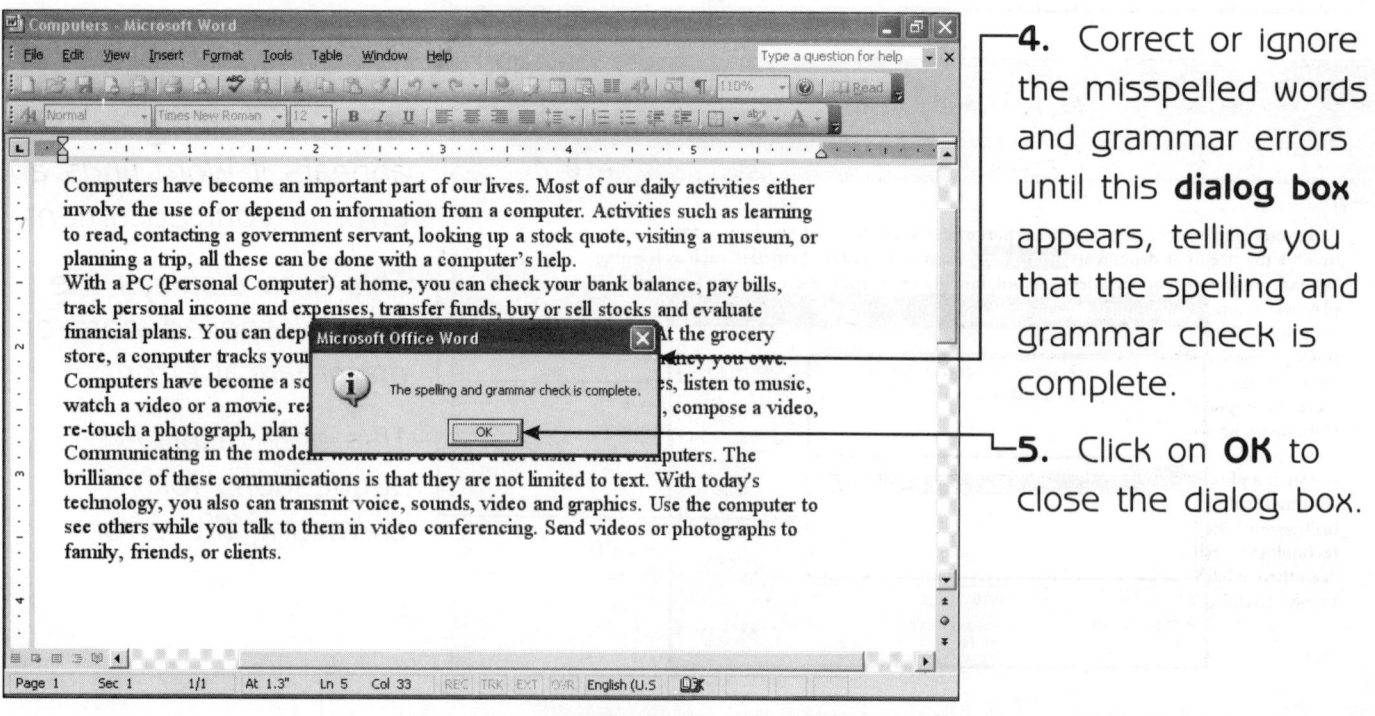

4. Correct or ignore the misspelled words and grammar errors until this **dialog box** appears, telling you that the spelling and grammar check is complete.

5. Click on **OK** to close the dialog box.

Word

Inserting Symbols

You can also insert symbols, into your document from the menu bar.

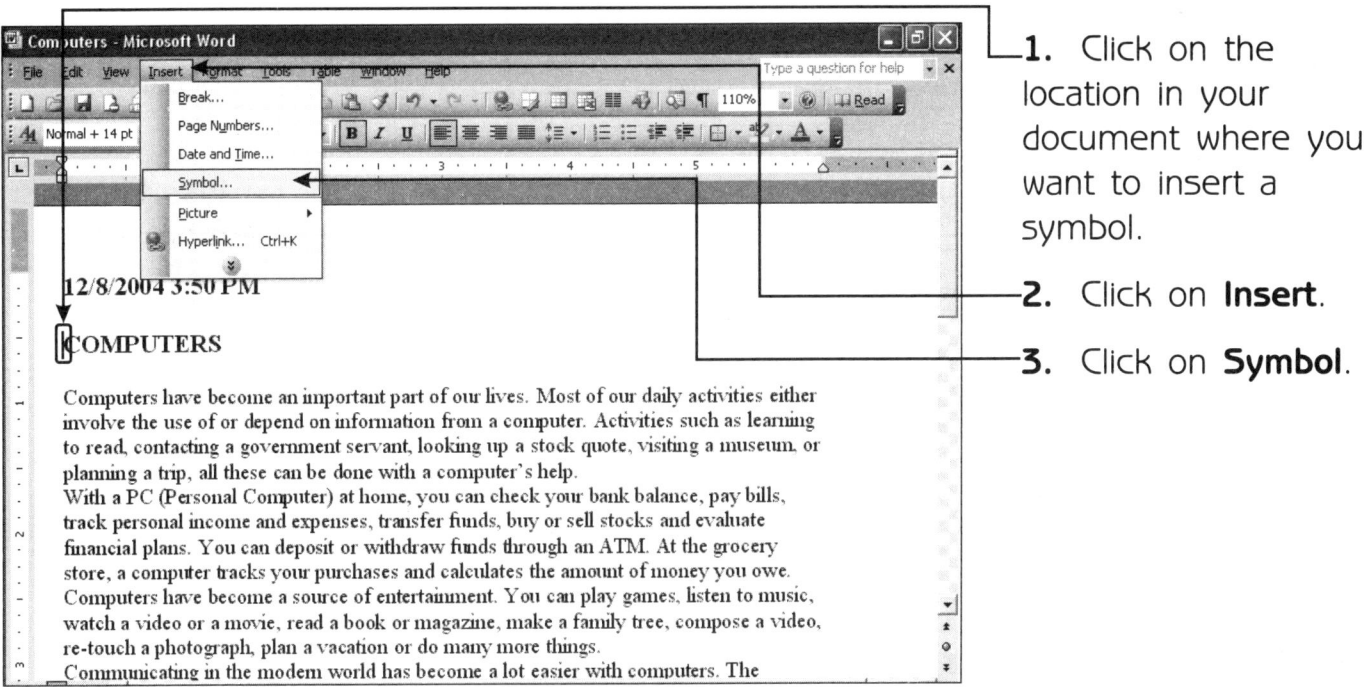

1. Click on the location in your document where you want to insert a symbol.

2. Click on **Insert**.

3. Click on **Symbol**.

The **Symbol** dialog box appears, displaying the symbols for the current font.

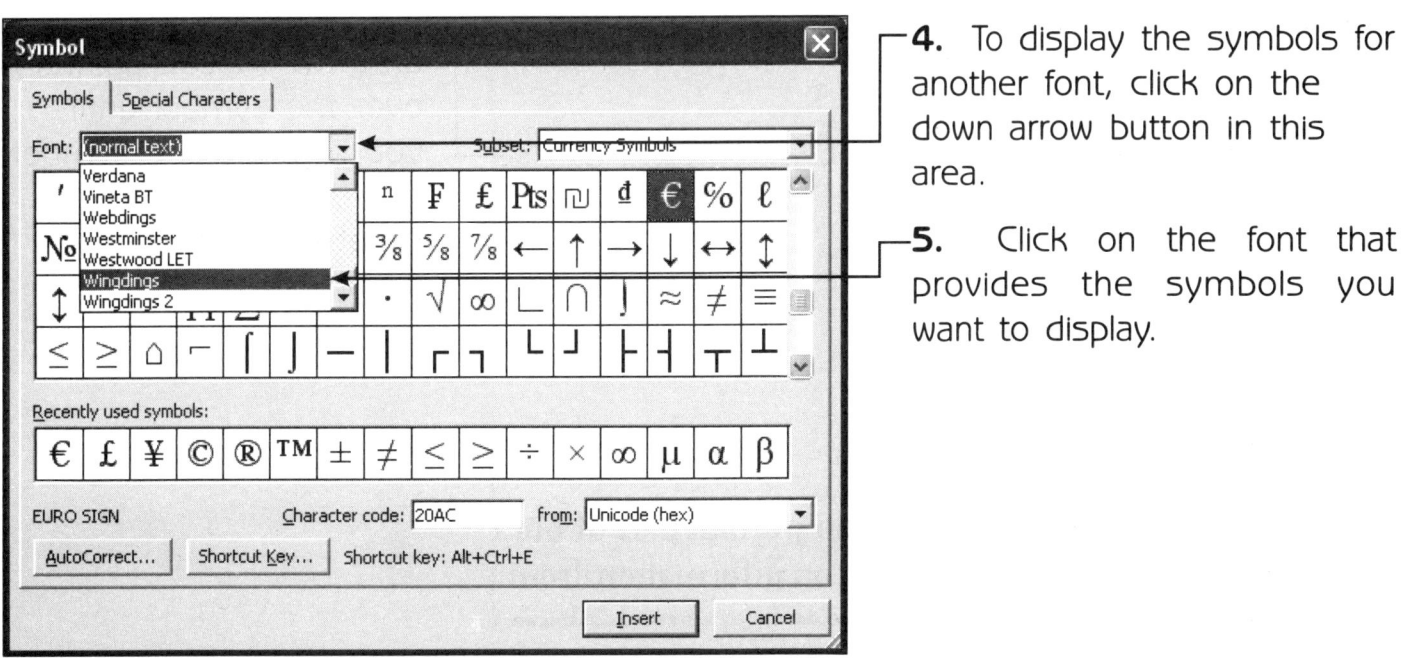

4. To display the symbols for another font, click on the down arrow button in this area.

5. Click on the font that provides the symbols you want to display.

29

Drag and Drop Series

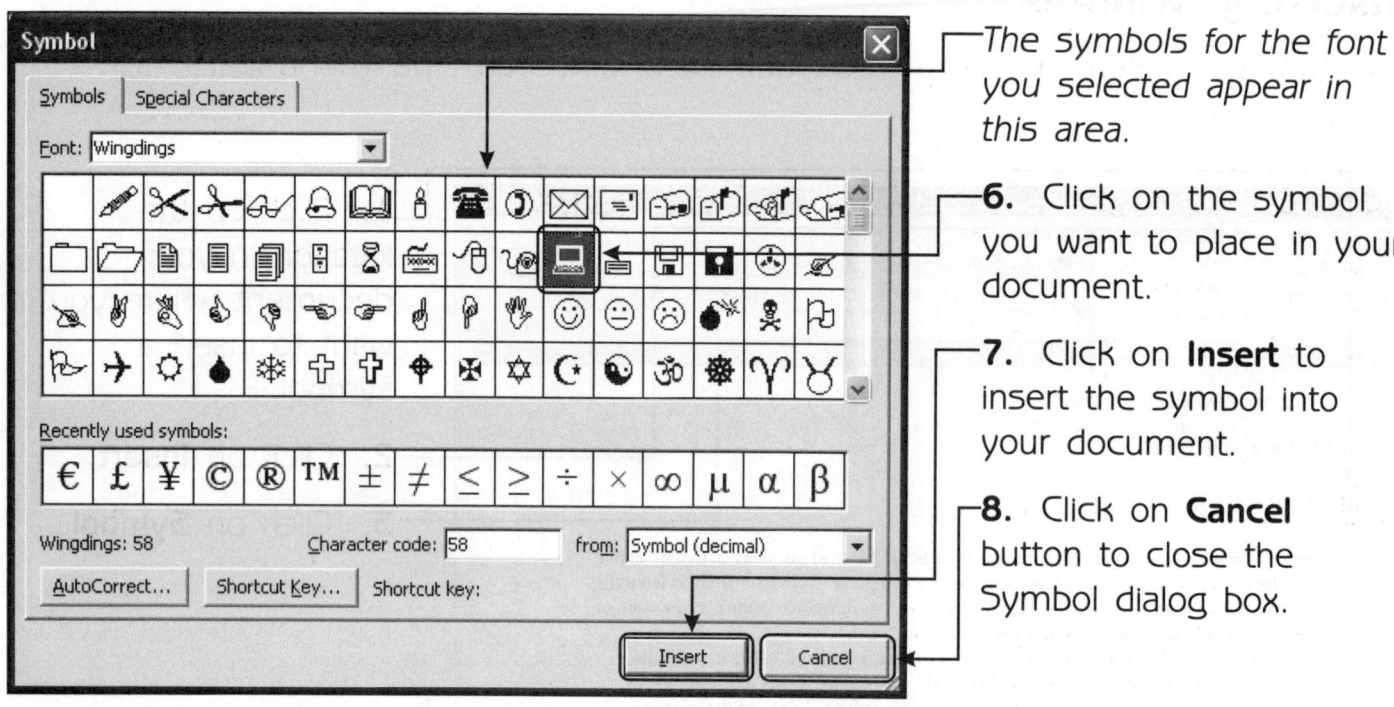

The symbols for the font you selected appear in this area.

6. Click on the symbol you want to place in your document.

7. Click on **Insert** to insert the symbol into your document.

8. Click on **Cancel** button to close the Symbol dialog box.

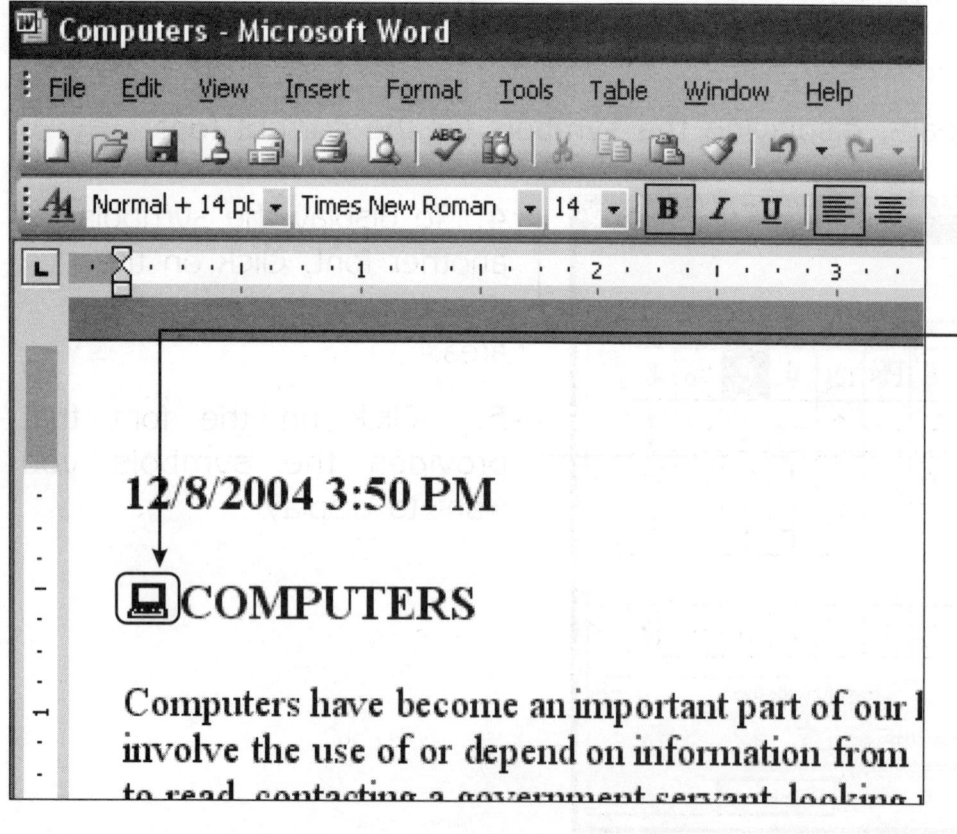

The symbol appears in your document.

To remove a symbol from your document, drag the mouse pointer over the symbol until you highlight the symbol and then, press the **Delete** key on the keyboard.

30

4. Formatting the Text

Changing the Font of the Text

You can change the font of the text to enhance the appearance of your document.

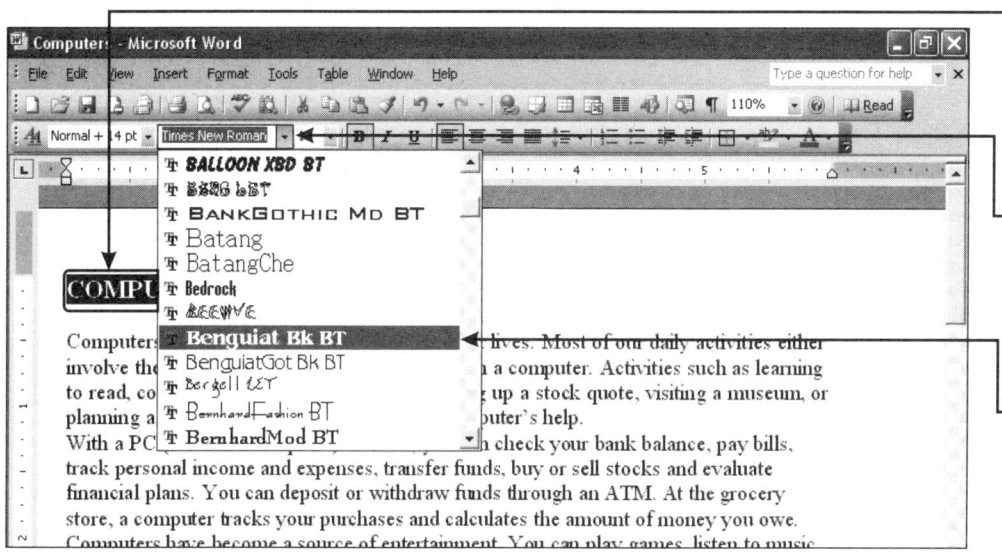

1. Select the text you want to change to a different font.

2. Click on the down arrow button to display a list of the available fonts.

3. Click on the font you want to use.

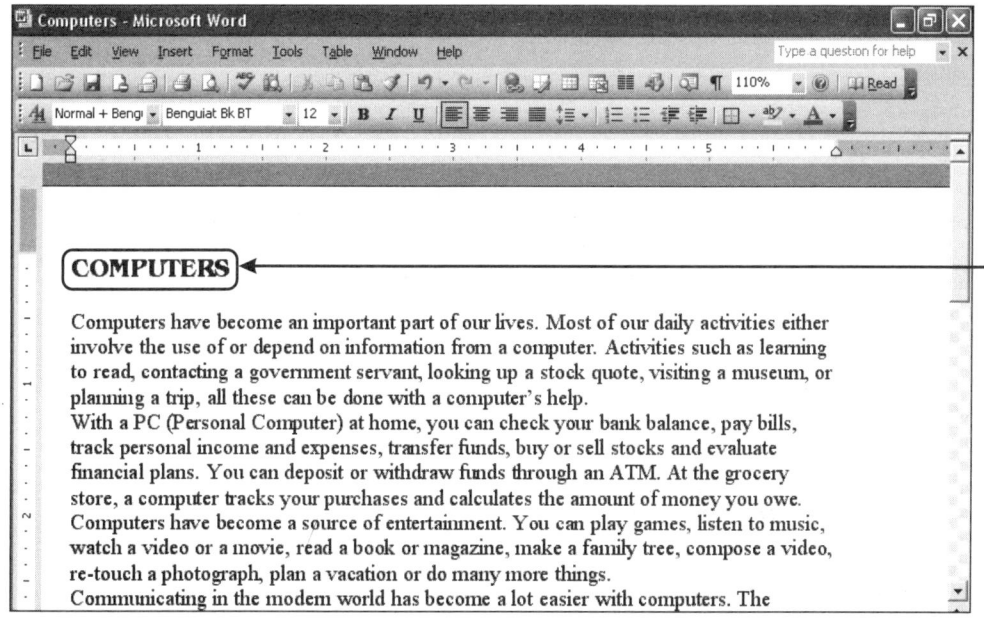

The text you selected changes to the new font.

To deselect the text, click outside the selected area.

Drag and Drop Series

Changing the Size of the Text

You can increase or decrease the size of the text in your document.

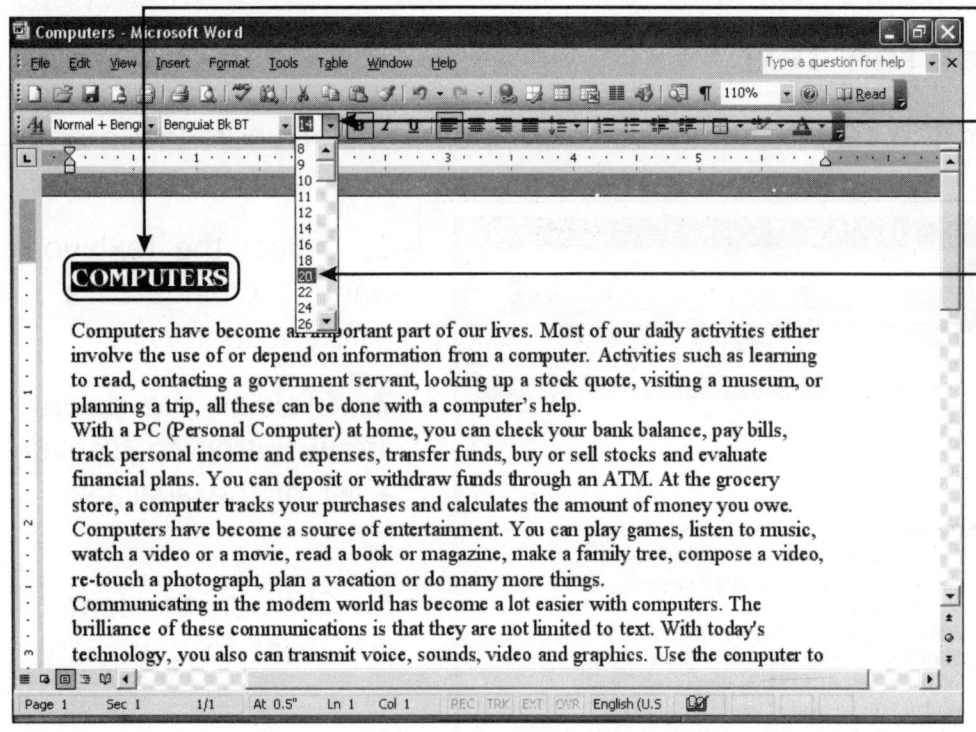

1. Select the text you want to change to a new size.

2. Click on the down arrow button to display a list of the available sizes.

3. Click on the size you want to use.

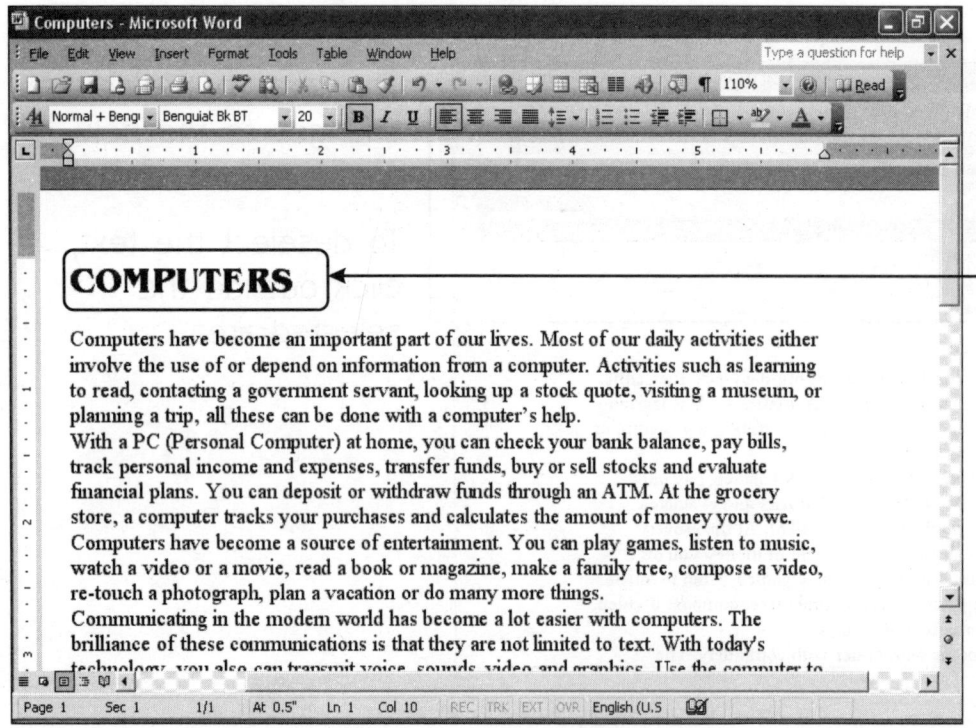

The text you selected changes to the new size.

To deselect the text, click outside the selected area.

Word

Changing the Text to Bold, Italic or Underline

You can make your text bold or italicize it or underline it to hiighlight the information in your document.

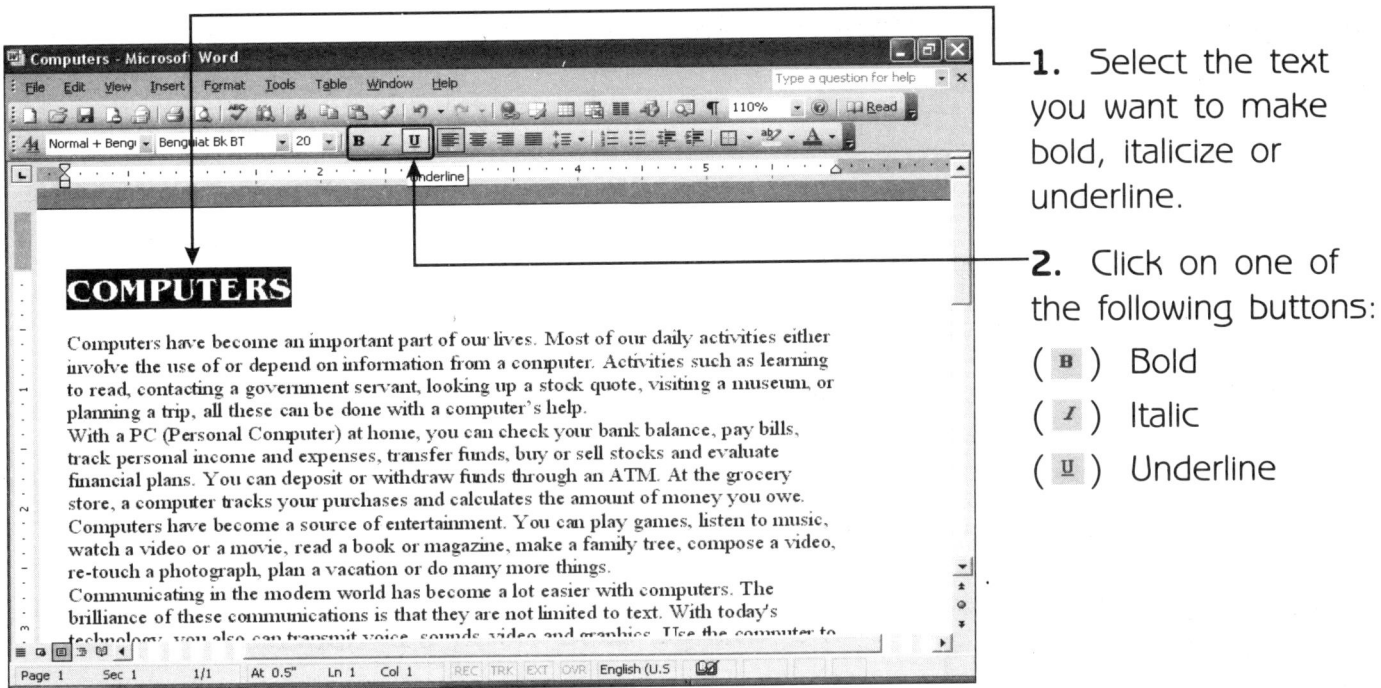

1. Select the text you want to make bold, italicize or underline.

2. Click on one of the following buttons:
   (**B**) Bold
   (*I*) Italic
   (U) Underline

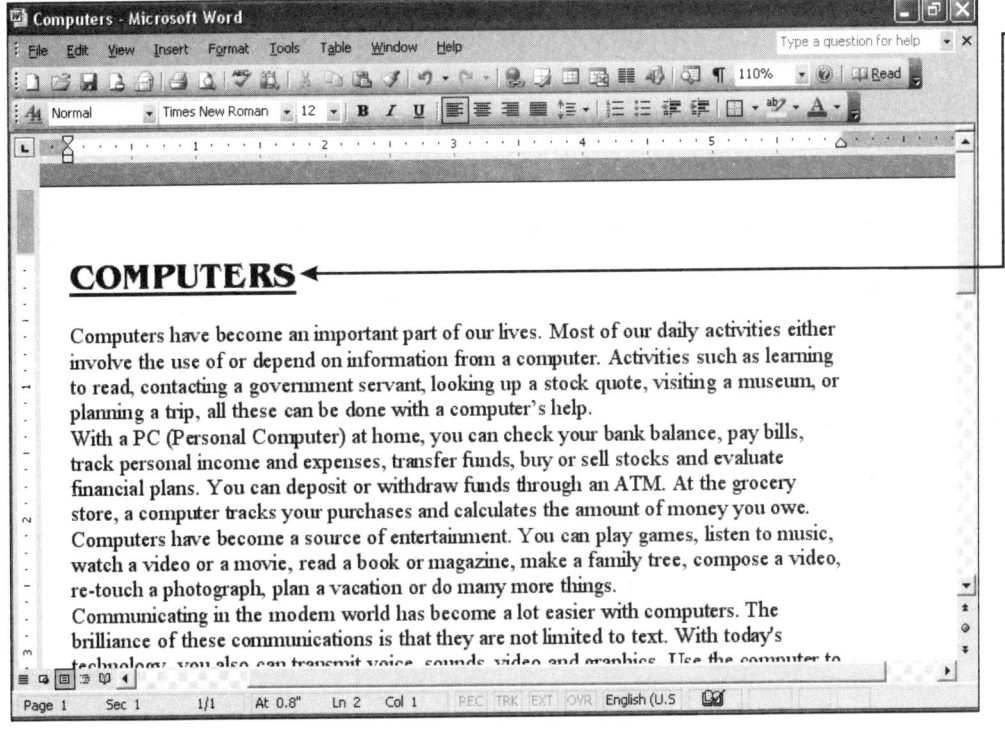

The text you selected appears in the new style.

To deselect the text, click outside the selected area.

To remove the bold, italic or underline style, repeat steps 1 and 2.

33

Drag and Drop Series

Changing the Case

You can change the case of the text in your document without retyping the text. Word offers five case styles to choose from.

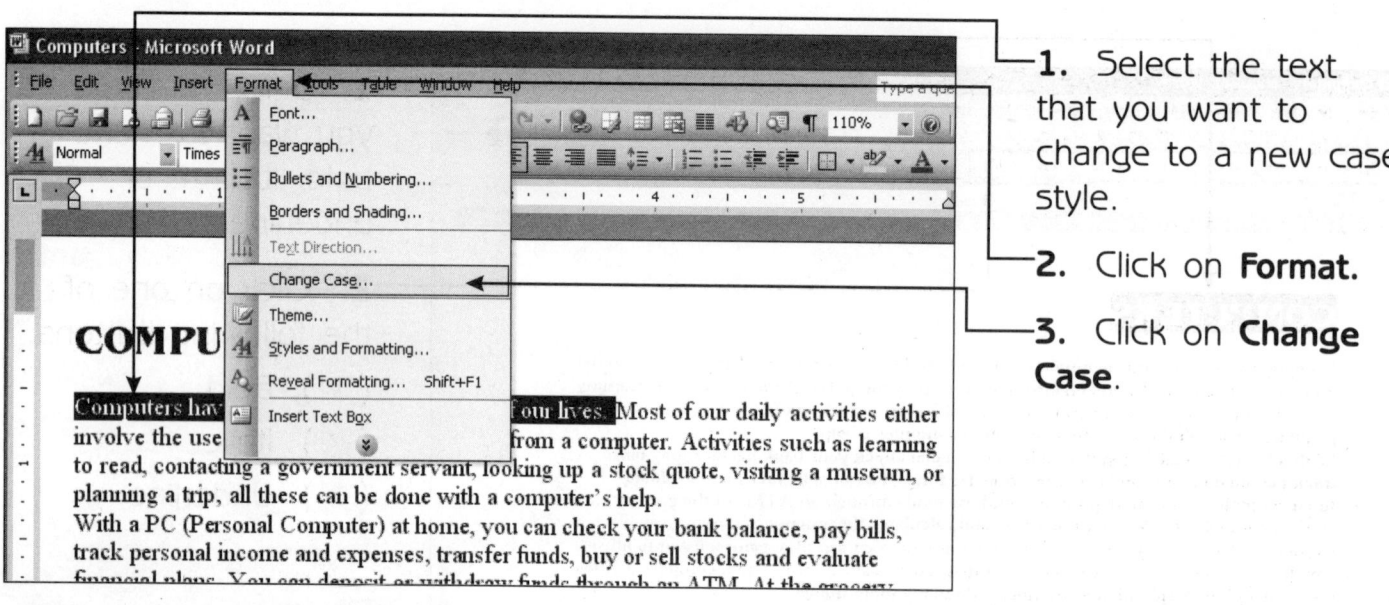

1. Select the text that you want to change to a new case style.

2. Click on **Format**.

3. Click on **Change Case**.

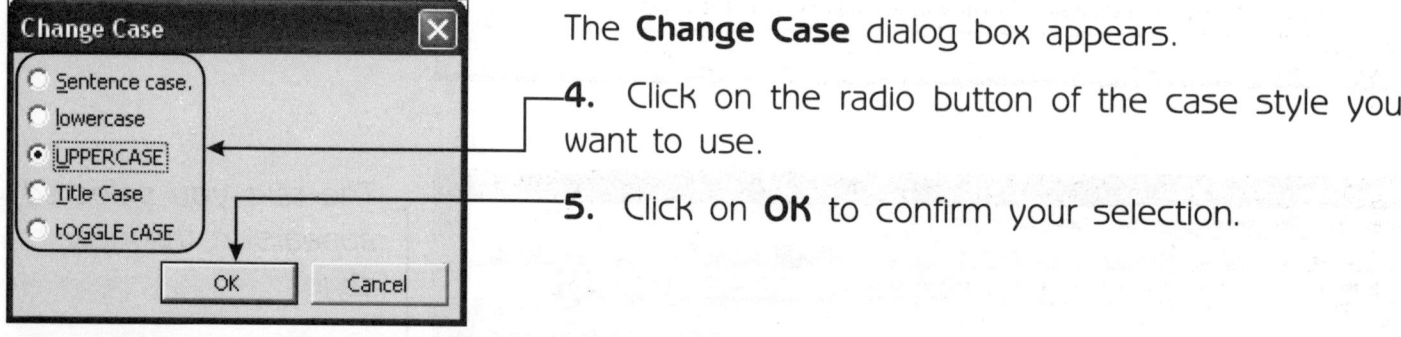

The **Change Case** dialog box appears.

4. Click on the radio button of the case style you want to use.

5. Click on **OK** to confirm your selection.

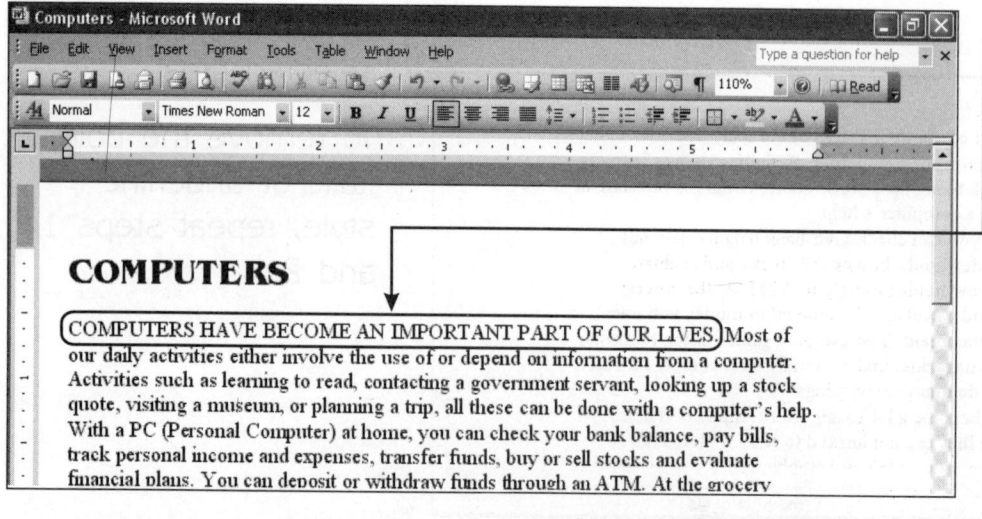

The text you selected changes to the new case style.

To deselect the text, click outside the selected area.

Word

Changing the Color of the Text

Color of the text can be changed to draw attention to headings or important information in your document.

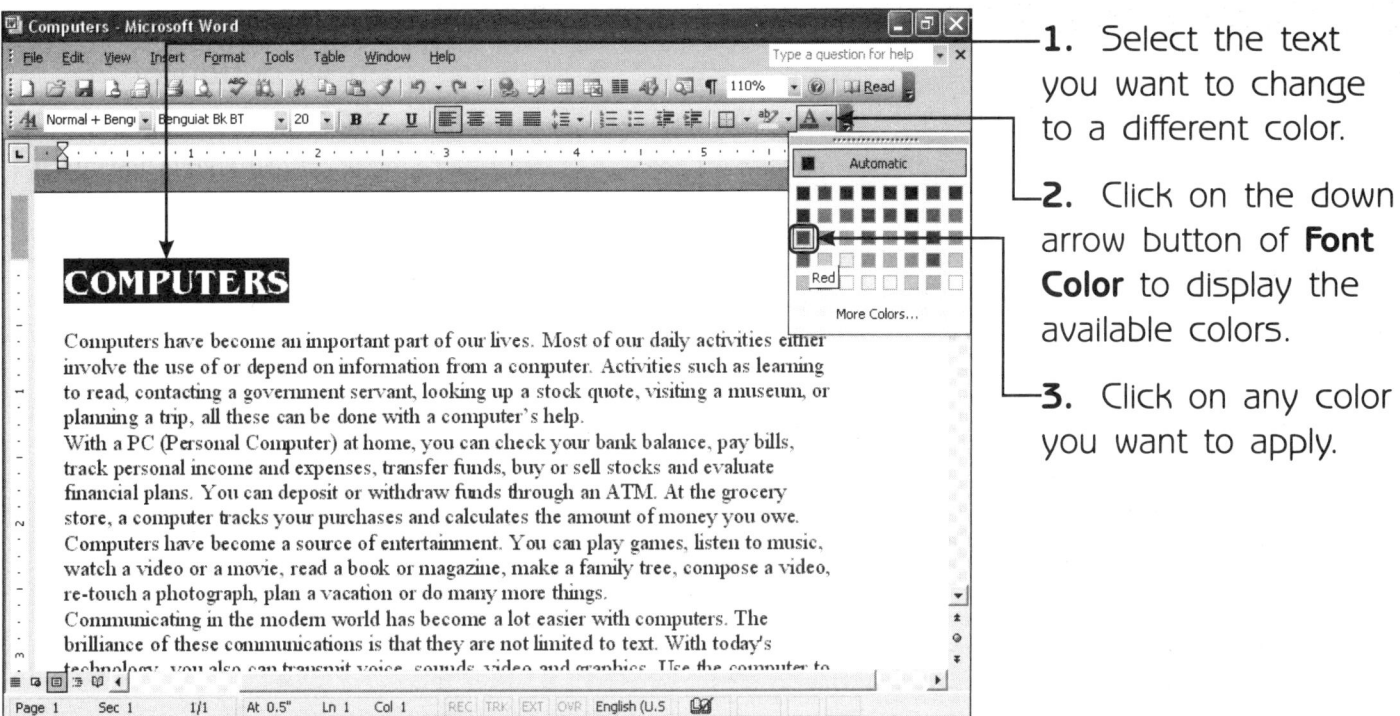

1. Select the text you want to change to a different color.

2. Click on the down arrow button of **Font Color** to display the available colors.

3. Click on any color you want to apply.

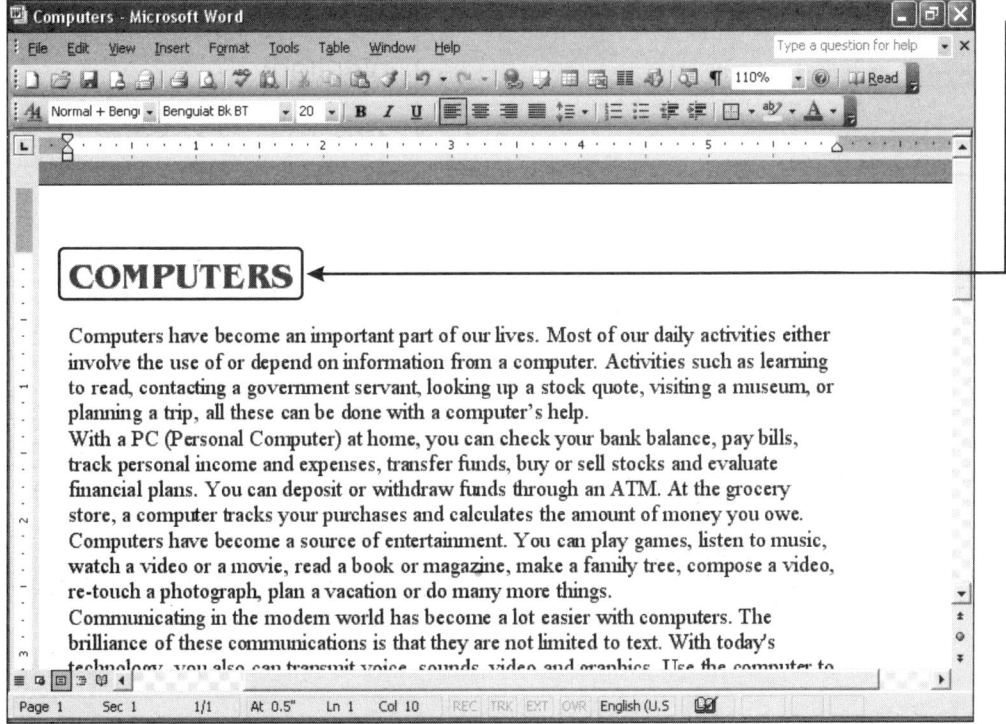

The text appears in the color you selected.

To deselect, click outside the selected area.

To return the text to its original color, repeat steps **1** to **3**, selecting **Automatic** in step **3**.

Drag and Drop Series

Highlighting the Text

Text can be highlighted so that it looks different in your document. Highlighting text is useful for marking information you want to review or verify later.

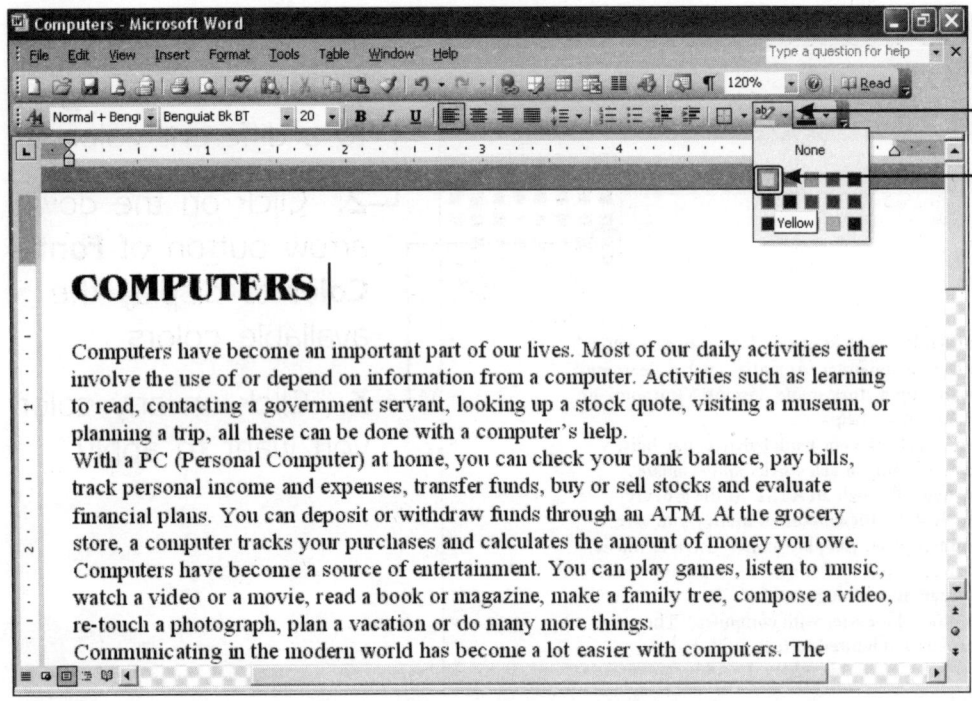

1. Click on the down arrow button of **Highlight** to display the available highlight colors.

2. Click on any color you want to use.

The mouse pointer changes to ( ) when placed over the document.

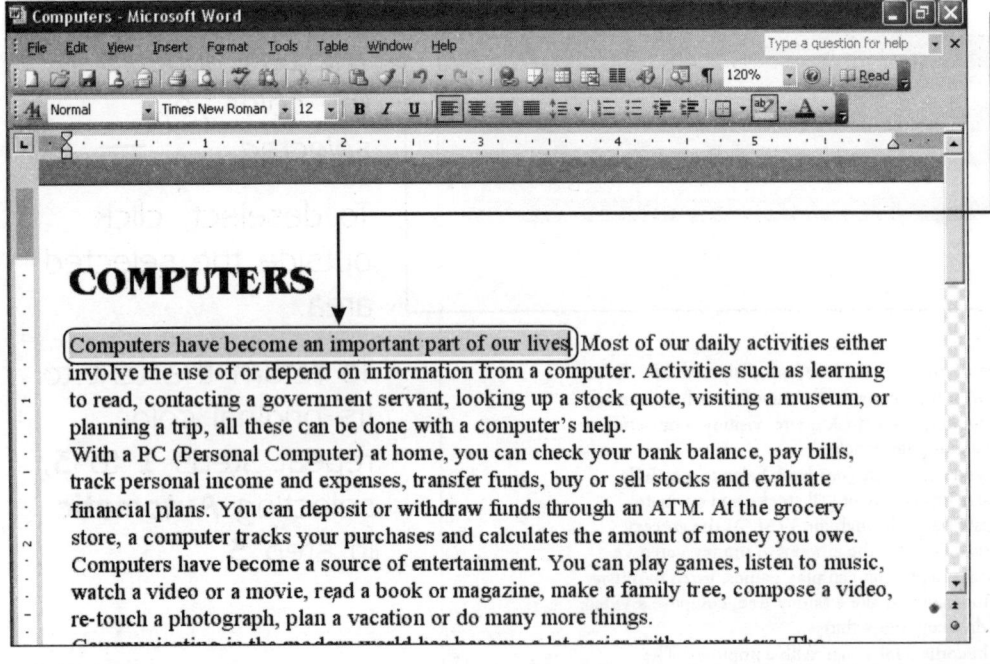

3. Select the area of the text you want to highlight.

The text you select appears highlighted.

4. When you finish highlighting the text, press the **Esc** key on the keyboard.

To remove highlighting from the selected text, repeat steps **1** to **4**, selecting **None** in step **2**.

Word

Changing the Alignment of the Text

You can align the text in different ways to enhance the appearance of your document.

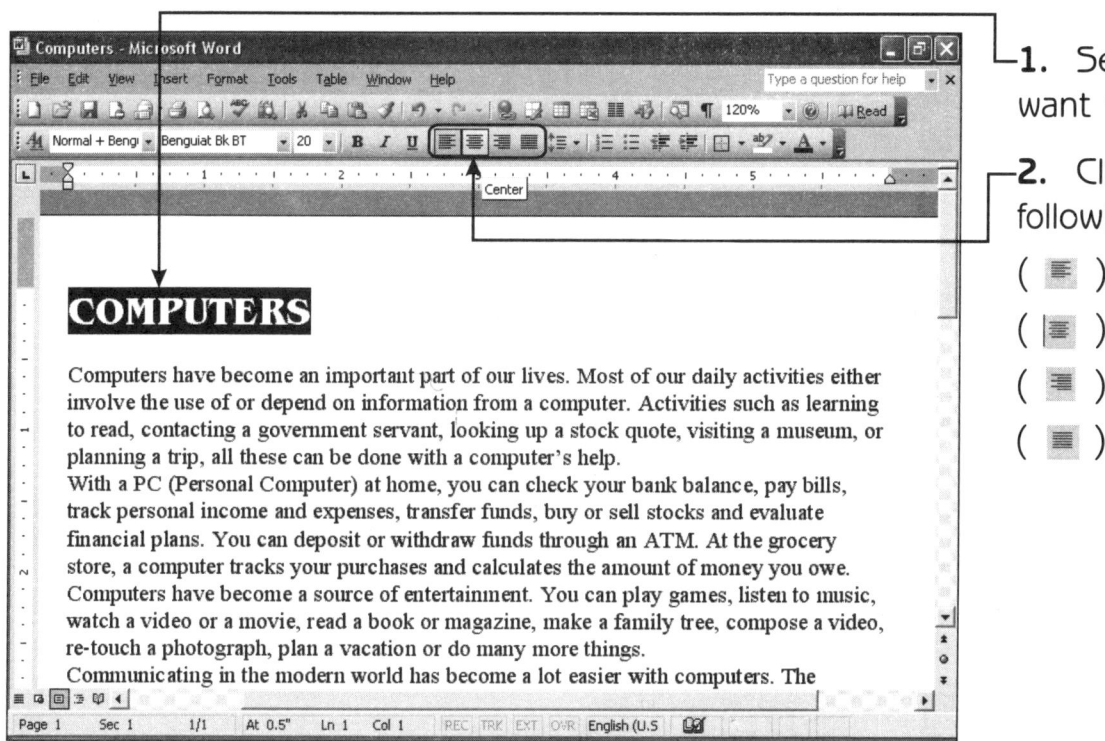

1. Select the text you want to align differently.

2. Click on one of the following buttons.

   (≡) Left align
   (≡) Center
   (≡) Right align
   (≡) Justify

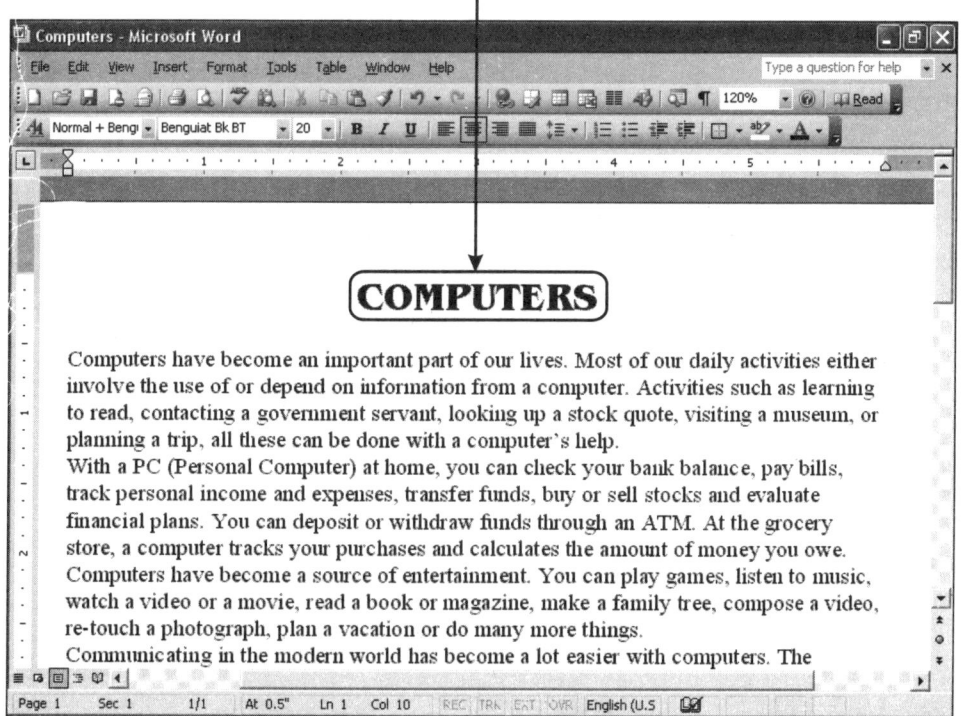

The text displays the new alignment.

To deselect the text, click outside the selected area.

Drag and Drop Series

Adding WordArt

You can add WordArt to your document to display a decorative title or draw attention to important information.

1. Click on the location in your document where you want to add WordArt.
2. Click on **Insert**.
3. Click on **Picture**.
4. Click on **WordArt**.

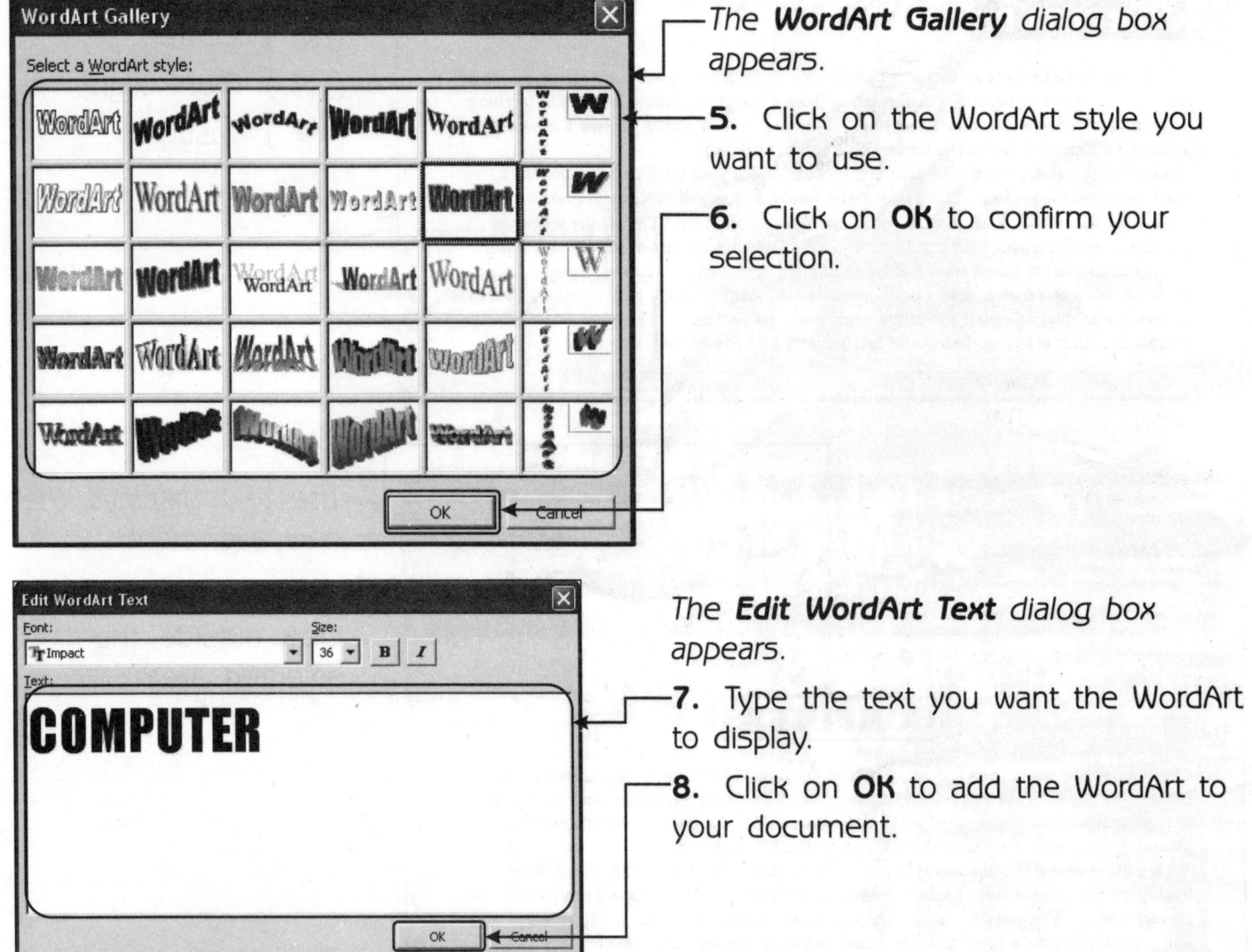

*The **WordArt Gallery** dialog box appears.*

5. Click on the WordArt style you want to use.

6. Click on **OK** to confirm your selection.

*The **Edit WordArt Text** dialog box appears.*

7. Type the text you want the WordArt to display.

8. Click on **OK** to add the WordArt to your document.

The **WordArt** appears in your document.

Word

Creating a Table

You can create and insert a table to neatly display information in your document.

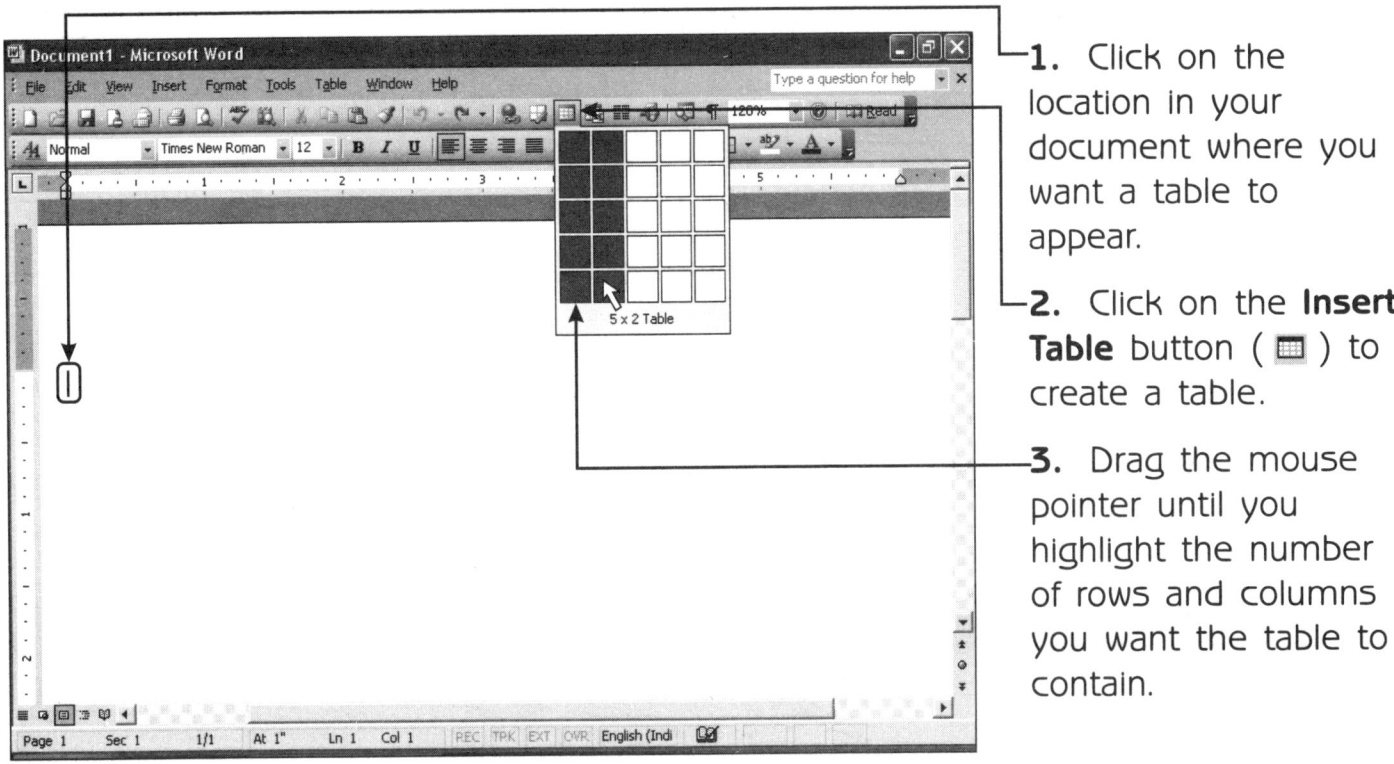

1. Click on the location in your document where you want a table to appear.

2. Click on the **Insert Table** button (▦) to create a table.

3. Drag the mouse pointer until you highlight the number of rows and columns you want the table to contain.

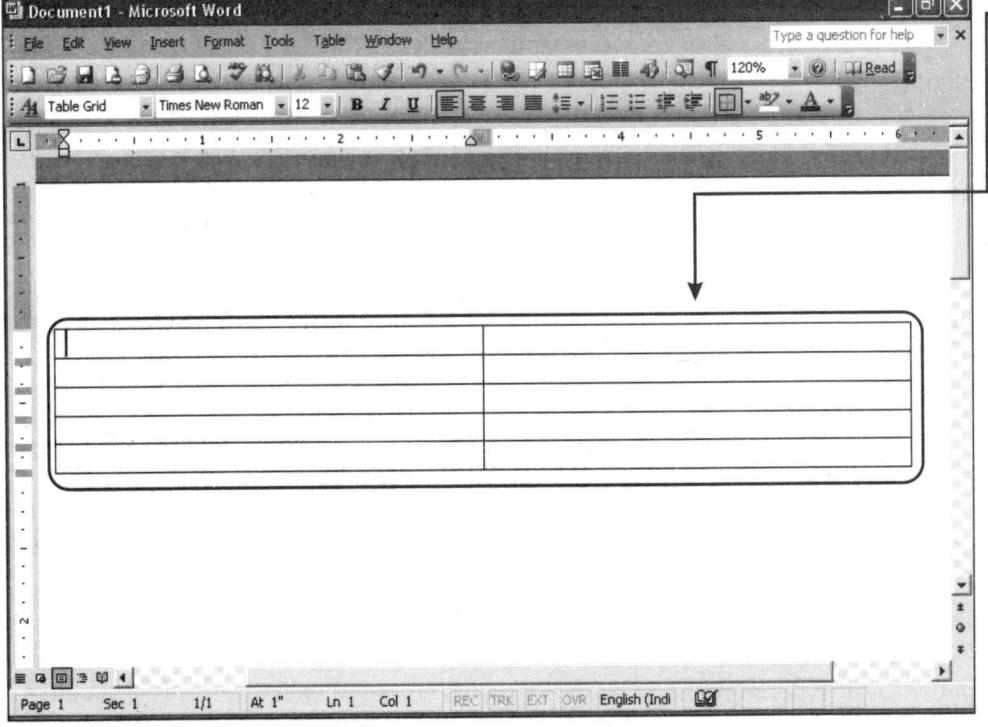

The table appears in your document.

39

Drag and Drop Series

To Enter Text in a Table

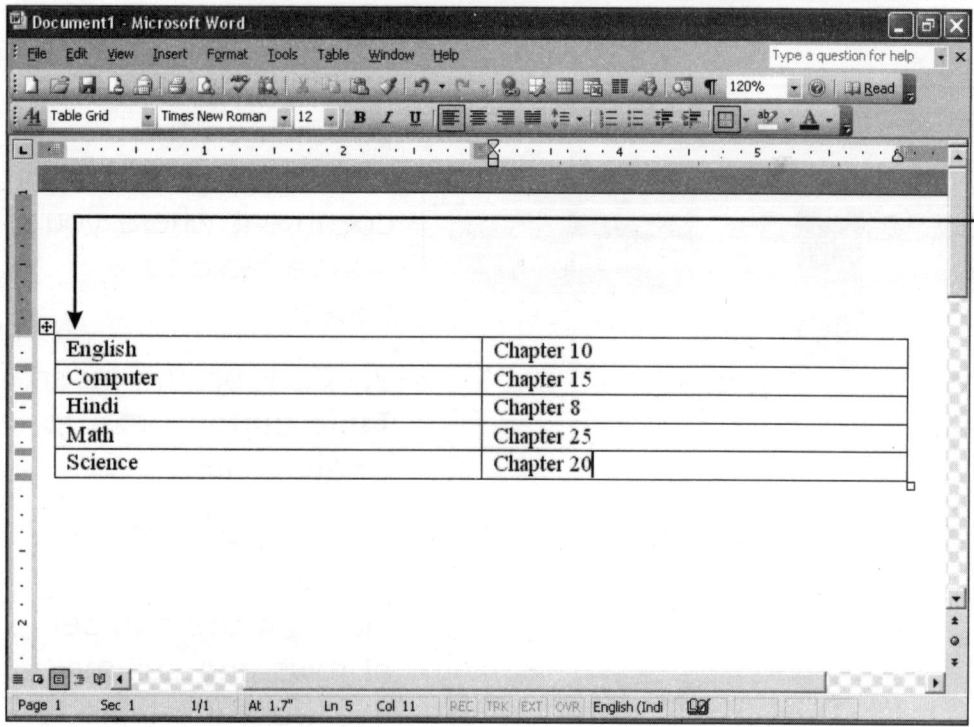

1. Click on the cell where you want to enter the text. Then type the text.

2. Repeat step **1** until you finish entering all the text for the table.

To Delete a Table

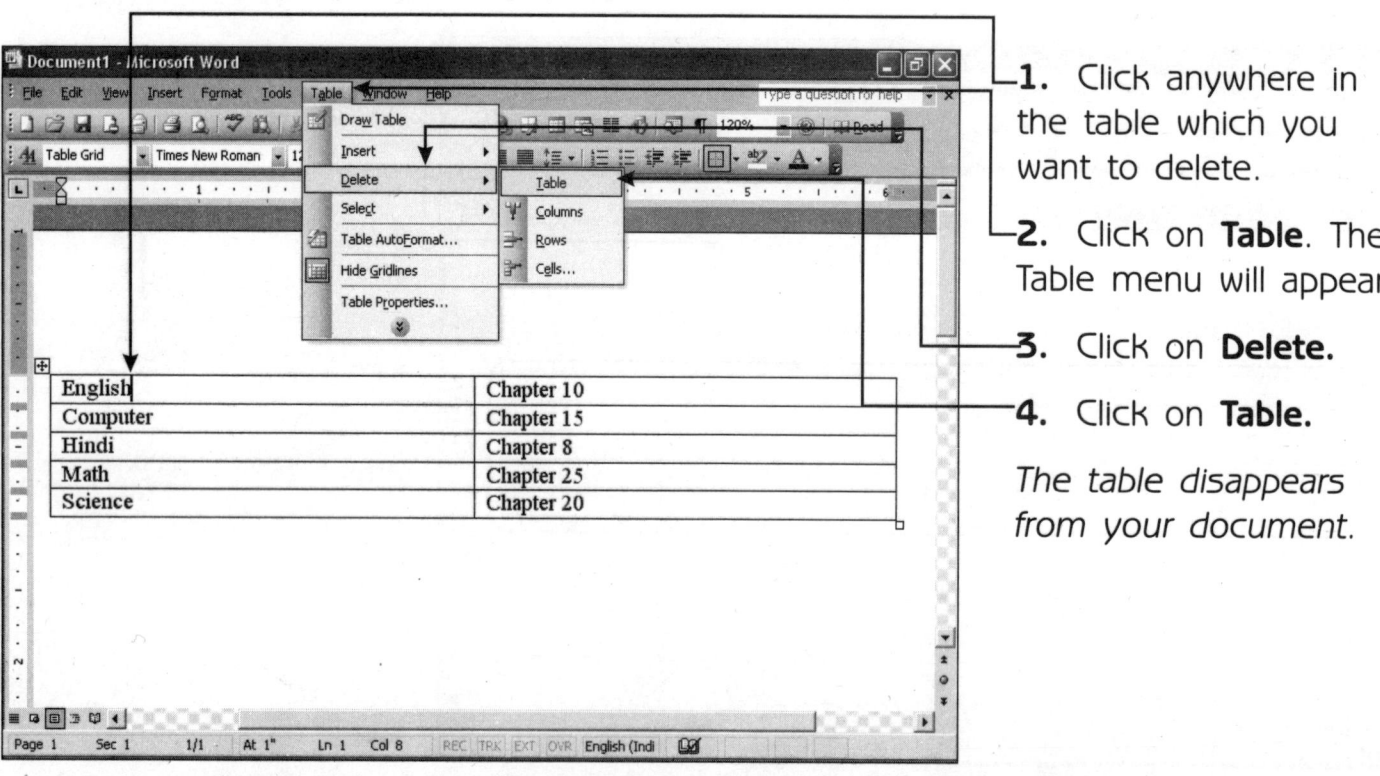

1. Click anywhere in the table which you want to delete.

2. Click on **Table**. The Table menu will appear.

3. Click on **Delete**.

4. Click on **Table**.

The table disappears from your document.

40